OTHER BOOKS BY DIANE HARVEY:

DOCTOR, PATIENT, OBJECT, THING:
A Story about a Surgeon and a Teacher

SOUL SURGERY
A STORY ABOUT TRANSCENDING TRAUMA

Diane Anderson Harvey, Ph.D.

AuthorHouse™
1663 Liberty Drive, Suite 200
Bloomington, IN 47403
www.authorhouse.com
Phone: 1-800-839-8640

This book is a work of non-fiction. Unless otherwise noted, the author and the publisher make no explicit guarantees as to the accuracy of the information contained in this book and in some cases, names of people and places have been altered to protect their privacy.

© 2007 Diane Anderson Harvey, Ph.D.. All rights reserved.

No part of this book may be reproduced, stored in a retrieval system, or transmitted by any means without the written permission of the author.

First published by AuthorHouse 12/11/2007

ISBN: 978-1-4343-3795-5 (sc)

Printed in the United States of America
Bloomington, Indiana

This book is printed on acid-free paper.

Dedicated to all teachers who spend their lives encouraging the growth and development of others,

especially

Donald and Phyllis Anderson

Amelia Rathbun

Anthony Robbins

and

The Faculty of Menlo College

Acknowledgements

I have had the good fortune of having wonderful teachers in my life. Those whom I remember the most taught me more than academic skills or knowledge. They taught me that I had unique and special gifts and that I was to use them somehow to contribute to the progress of the world. None of them were cynics, all of them believed in people and progress. I doubt that their message was for me alone. It is likely that many of their students carried away with them the sense that they were unique and important, and that they had special responsibilities to carry out in their lives.

I come from a teaching family and I often observed my mother and father at work, my father's gentle but certain encouragement of those who had no sense of personal destiny and my mother's magical inspiration of the very souls of little children. These two people did not earn much money, as unfortunately is the case with most teachers, but they did not seem to notice that. Our small home near the beach was filled with love and laughter and ideas. My brother and I each began life under the care and guidance of two of the most remarkable teachers.

From Crown Point Elementary School to Pacific Beach Junior High School to Mission Bay High School—none of them fancy—to San

Diego State University, University of California at Berkeley, and Stanford University I can remember individual teachers who made me a better person as they encouraged my thirst for knowledge: Peter Dzerzipilsky, Jack Good, William Shepherd, Dr. Alan Shields, Dr. Alan Anderson, Dr. William Povenmire, Dr. Philip Rhinelander, and Dr. Stephen Krasner.

I also had the pleasure of observing excellent teaching as it touched the lives of my children at Nueva Learning Center and Crystal Springs Uplands School, two educational institutions that understood and valued the growth and contributions of both their teachers and their students. Among the many teachers in my memory are George Mason, Mary Laycock, Kent Holubar, Tom Woosnam, Rod Jacobson, Norma Fifer, Nancy Rosenthal, John Neuburger, and Stephen Weislogel.

Not all teachers are found in educational institutions. The Foster City sports teams provided us with Ron and Jack Allen who coached football and helped young boys grow up. "Coach" Sorensen coached football and also taught karate. Chuck Philips found time to coach football, basketball, and baseball while raising his own young sons alone. The Boy Scouts sent teachers in our direction as well, starting with my husband, Dave, who was Scoutmaster for fifteen years, and the wonderful men who assisted him.

My almost quarter of a century at Menlo College, which hires teachers for their love of teaching and their ability to teach, allowed me the privilege of watching master teachers at work. I acknowledge all of them and am grateful to have spent so much of my life among them.

Finally, teachers have arrived in my life when I was ready to move forward in consciousness. The two most influential were Amelia Rathbun and Anthony Robbins. These two people are true masters of both life and teaching. They each have an astonishing insight into other people and into the meaning of human life, which insight is aligned with a delivery that brings many people to them.

Three Menlo College colleagues whom I highly regard took time not only to read the manuscript for this book, but to enter into dialogue about the import of what I have said. I greatly appreciate the thoughts of Dr. Eugene Bales, Professor of Philosophy; Dr. Craig Medlen, Professor of Economics; and Dr. Marilyn Thomas, Professor of Literature. Dr. Thomas has been most generous with her time and talent in making sure that this book makes sense to the reader and that it is easy to read. I also thank Dr. Tim Kochems and Pam McCormick who as professionals in the field of psychology took time from their busy schedules to contribute their expertise and their comments and suggestions regarding the ideas in the manuscript.

My special friends Janet Grant, Suzette Rennison, and Kelly Stahl, were with me as readers once again, as was my husband, Dave Harvey. I welcome Pat Crawford, Diana Huang, and Debbie Shaw as new readers. Readers give the wonderful gift of time and honest assessment and well deserve the appreciation that I have for their contribution to this book.

With all of these teachers in my life, it would seem that this should be the perfect book, but there surely will be errors and omissions. If either the ideas or the writing show signs of error or oversight, that is solely my responsibility.

Diane Anderson Harvey
San Mateo, California
August, 2007

Contents

Foreword.. xiii
Introduction For The Reader.................... xvii

PREPARING

Song Of The Soul 3
I Can't Go Back..................................5
Riptide 9
Reason To The Rescue............................13
Circles Of Knowledge............................17
First-circle Sensory Knowledge 19
Second-circle Rational Knowledge................23
Third-circle Knowledge By Faith 27
Fourth-circle Knowledge Through Personal Insight 33
Which Circle?...................................37
Connections 39

DIAGNOSING

Images And Symbols..............................45
The Private Place (Creativity) 49
The Breath Of Life (Spirituality) 55
The View From A Gurney (Reason And Emotion) 57
The Surgeon (Passionate Intensity) 61
The Intuition (Destiny).........................67
The Sadness (Disappointment)....................71
The Loneliness (Existential Disconnection)......81
The Abandonment (Independence) 85
Guidelines (Joining The Symbols)................91

OPERATING

External Pressure 99
Your Time Is Up 103
Hurry Up 109
The Transition 113
Trust 117
The Decision 123
The Act 129
The Response 133
Done 137
No Need To Look Back 141

HEALING

Leap Of Faith 145
Being 149

Foreword

If you are reading this, you—or perhaps someone you are trying to help—probably know the following experience: Shock, and our lives—as we knew them moments ago—suddenly and unexpectedly begin to change. The change is not pleasant, but dreadful. It is overwhelming. We are overwhelmed by disruptive events, relationships, and emotions. For many of us, it would only have been through nightmares that any of these events or emotions would have come into our lives earlier.

It is difficult enough suffering through that kind of shock and overwhelm. As most of us know, it is also hard work to find some stability. Diane Anderson Harvey's earlier book, *Doctor, Patient, Object, Thing*, is her own story of shock, overwhelm, and efforts at coming through them to some new, positive physical and relational stability.

In *Soul Surgery: A Story about Transcending Trauma* Diane Anderson Harvey goes much further. She does something many of us don't bother to try to do. It is a gift to us that she shares her story, giving us the details of her process. For most of us it is enough just to get through fear and suffering and then gradually deal with our new status quo. In this book, Diane tells the story of desiring more. She desires more emotional healing and understanding—a greater sense of life post-trauma. In order to obtain more healing and life, she searches for the meaning in her experience.

She searches relentlessly and systematically for three months. Her search illustrates the stunning capacities of our human organism: how responsive our mind, body, feelings, and spirits are to each other and to our world, and how much integration is possible among mind, body, emotions, and spirit. Hers is a very detailed and systematically drawn illustration. It is very human. It is hers. As she stresses throughout her book, there are many paths on which to search for meaning. Diane traveled the path most available and reliable to her, an intellectual and intuitive one, and yet she was wonderfully open to discovering and developing more. She responded to her trauma with what she had available to her. Without doubt it is an approach that demonstrates the value of a liberal arts college education. At the hands of a master educator, we see how that kind of education can be fruitfully applied and how it leads to greater openness to self and life. However, we all start with where we are and who we are. Using what we have, we are challenged to develop more.

Diane's story, her search for meaning, is a spiritual journey. It is that way for all of us. It is not just about her own conscious personal desire for personal meaning. She was almost literally called to it through an intuition that said, "Don't go back!" An intuition that came from somewhere beyond her conscious self. But she, like all of us, was also called to it through emotions and events. We all exclaim, "Why me? Why now? Why so painful?" However, those exclamations are actually questions and it seems Diane experienced them as calling for answers. She discerned the answers and tested their quality using her abilities and experience—her awareness, intelligence, relationships, feelings, and intuitions.

Since I have been immersed in recent years in appreciating the life and spirituality of the Catholic saint Ignatius of Loyola, I cannot help but find aspects of his life and *Spiritual Exercises* resonating in a non-religious way with Professor Harvey's life and method. He began his own search for a different kind of meaning while recovering from a near fatal war injury and its consequences. He was continually asking and looking for more meaning in his life, always "more." Most fundamentally, he would have appreciated Professor Harvey's systematic intellectual and intuitive method. He insisted that God could be discerned in all things, and so he explicitly encouraged the use of our intellects, intuitions, feelings, and the knowledge of the world available to us. As the founder of the Jesuits, it was this foundational insight that guided them to develop universities throughout the world. The Jesuits and Professor Harvey value and use their significant academic and professional training but will not be limited by it—will not let it silence intuition or feelings. Most evocatively for me, it is my sense that Diane Anderson Harvey illustrates in her book an approach to the search for meaning and a testing of its fruits that Ignatius called "discernment"—in his perspective, trying to understand where God, in God's love for us, is leading us based on all the cues our humanness can bring to our awareness. It is a search for meaning and vocation that could not be more human.

In fact, what I was most impressed with in Diane Anderson Harvey's story was its humanness and her courage—to be open to her experience, learn from it, even discern it, and now to share it. She shares it in a voice that is clear and easy, not heavy. As told in this book, her own search for meaning was successful. She did experience greater emotional healing and increased understanding. The search did lead her to something different and, we must assume, "more" in her life. Her story encourages us all to do the same in our own lives, develop more, by starting when we can, where we are, with who we are, and in our own way.

Tim Kochems, Ph.D.
Clinical Psychologist and Psychoanalyst
Faculty, Boston Psychoanalytic Society and Institute
Faculty, Boston Institute for Psychotherapy
Private Practice, Newton Centre, MA
Formerly, for 25 years, Clinical Instructor in Psychology, Harvard Medical School

Introduction For The Reader

This is a book about responding to unexpected, unusual, and traumatic experiences in life. It is a story, actually, of my attempt as a thinker to respond to such an experience. My unexpected experience came in the guise of a rare female surgery, but such experiences could also include losses of jobs, deaths of loved ones, burning down of houses, spousal affairs, children's serious illnesses, economic setbacks and any other fracture of the usual activities of life.

My style for taking command of the experience involved thinking. Other people, with other approaches to life, other styles of living, might respond through different creative endeavors, by painting, perhaps, or composing, or dancing, or building things, by writing or gardening.

Though I am a trained philosopher, and though in this chronicle of events I occasionally refer to well-known philosophers, this is not a philosophical work in the formal sense. It is more akin to poetry, perhaps even to mysticism as one of my most respected philosophy colleagues has suggested. Somewhere in the story, I distinguish among several ways of knowing: knowing from sensory experience, knowing from reason, knowing from faith, and knowing from personal insights. Since I am by nature a thinker and an intuitor, I sought to resolve my unexpected traumatic experience through reason and personal insight.

Though the approach that I used is rational in the sense that it is organized thought, it does not adhere to the tenets of contemporary formal logical analysis, certainly not to the rules of empiricism, and it is likely to stretch the patience of strict rationalists. My approach has more in common with the works of the so-called depth psychologists, especially with the works of Carl Jung.

My traumatic experience was not as much the diagnosis of disease and the ensuing surgery, but the experiences following the surgery: some surprising emotions, a compelling intuition, and an uncomfortable interaction with the surgeon. The interaction with the surgeon as well as the story of the surgery is chronicled in *DOCTOR, PATIENT, OBJECT, THING*; the story you are about to read tells how I, as a thinker-intuitor, addressed the emotions and the intuition.

There were two unsettling emotions—sadness and loneliness—and an intuition that simply, but powerfully, said I could not go back without telling me to what I could not go back. I wanted to get rid of negative emotions and interactions as quickly as possible, and I had to attend to the intuition in a timely fashion as well. I needed to resolve the two specific emotions and respond to the intuition before I could transcend the entire experience, but before I could overcome emotions and deal with intuitions I had to understand their purpose.

I decided, first, to use the surgical experience as a foundation from which I could seek the meaning of that experience for my life in general. Then, I adapted Jung's approach to dream analysis as my procedure. One of the differences between Freud's and Jung's approaches to dream analysis is that Jung, but not Freud, has the dreamer select the most important symbols in the dream and then has the dreamer draw meaningful associations from those symbols to the dreamer's life in general. In my approach to transcending my traumatic experience, I selected the most important images *to me* from the surgical experience, considered various symbols that seemed to be related to those chosen images, and then set about drawing associations between those symbols and other parts of my life.

I considered the symbols that were associated with my chosen images of the experience to be clues to my understanding of the emotions and intuition. I used the symbols to draw out my thoughts about the experience, the emotions, and the intuition in much the same way that a projective test draws out the subject's thoughts or world view. When I had done this for each of the symbols, I gathered my insights together and discovered a new way of looking at the meaning of the surgical experience for my life. I assumed that this understanding also would assist me in resolving the emotions and responding to the intuition. I was in for a surprise before that happened.

My approach clarified the emotions and the intuition and brought me to the point of a major life choice. It did not, however, provide me with the courage to make the choice. That came from somewhere else. It helped, though, that I had acknowledged and responded to the entire unexpected experience. Taking time to examine or reflect upon the possible meanings of such unusual or traumatic experiences seems contrary to the common wisdom of the times.

The common wisdom, especially in the worlds of medicine and employment, says to get over traumas as fast as possible. Get back home quickly, get back to work as soon as possible, get back to your normal life. Get on with it. Move on. Do not, under any circumstances, make important decisions in such unusual circumstances as traumatic experiences.

This story expresses my objection to that common wisdom. The story reveals my belief that there are various levels of life and that our "normal" life often is not the highest life available to us. I know that there are moments in life when we are knocked off our usual balance, our normalcy, and that from that vantage point we can view and interpret at a different level both life in general and our own lives in particular. Whether we subsequently change our lives for the better or simply note that there is more available to us than we have been experiencing, I think that our lives will be enriched. The common wisdom either deliberately or inadvertently discourages the use of traumatic experiences for deepening one's understanding or experience of life, and consequently reduces the potential such experiences have to enhance our lives; hence my story.

This is a simple story about one person's attempt to draw out the best from a difficult experience and to use a dramatic break in the regular routine of life as a learning experience about elevating one's life. My story is based upon a surgical experience and a thinker's approach to responding to it. If the opportunity comes to you, the reader, it is likely to come in some other form and you will approach it in your own way according to your nature and your talents. My message, however, is still the same. I encourage you to step into the experience, to be assured that there is meaning in it for you, to ask what you can learn from it, and to know that your life will be deepened by both the experience and your response to it.

Please also know that from some place, some time, I am cheering you on!

Diane Anderson Harvey

PREPARING

Song Of The Soul

The still small voice of intuition was not still and it was not small. It shouted. It commanded. It resonated throughout my entire body and left no possibility for my ignoring its presence. It came only once and in its single occurrence closed a chapter in my life.

I had made intuitive decisions before, but they had grown rather than erupted. By the time each of those decisions was made I was ready for it; I had wrapped it in a cloak of reason so that I could control the future change and could explain the decision to others.

Not so this time. This intuition was not a gradual unease that metamorphosed into a choice; it was a command to move on a moment's notice. The timing and the delivery of the intuition were perfect for catching my attention.

I was a rational person on a rational mission doing rational work and that fact played a major role in both the purpose of the intuition and in my response to it. At that moment, however, the moment of the intuition, I was not at my rational best. Having just emerged from a surgical procedure designed to save the skin graft from a prior surgery, I was physically and emotionally vulnerable. In that state, I did not have the usual rational resources to create or control my own future, and I was not able to explain to others where I would be going, only that I must go.

This does not mean that I did not *try* to rationally control the entire event. I did try—but I did not succeed. Many scholars argue that human motivation is based on emotion rather than reason, yet while there was certainly a lot of emotion involved in this experience, it was not the emotion that replaced reason and responded to the intuition; it was the life of the spirit—the song of the soul.

These pages describe a philosopher's response to an unexpected trauma and its attending emotions and intuition. The response to all three—the trauma, the emotions, and the intuition—involved a journey through and beyond both emotion and reason. The travelers on the journey included not only the philosopher, but also her companions, Fear and Trust. Only when Trust became more powerful than Fear was a decision made, the response completed, and the experience transcended. The moment of decision had nothing to do with reason or emotion. It was a response of the soul.

Before the response came the command.

The story begins with the command

I Can't Go Back

"I can't go back!" I heard it loud and clear. It was not a voice from outside, but it was not my voice either. It was not just my thoughts. It was knowledge that I had intuited somehow. It was a command.

It wasn't the whiney "I just can't do it" that we all have heard, or even expressed, in situations when someone has been stretched beyond his or her capacity or endurance and wants to give up.

"One more step," we respond then, or "One more time." "You can do it, just try. I will walk with you; I will wait with you while you try. I know you can do it. One more step, one more time, one more try, then we will stop and rest for a while."

It was not that "I can't."

I did not want to give up on anything.

Nor was it the "I can't go back" that implies I did not know how to get back.

I knew.

Neither was it the "I can't go back" that suggests going back would be embarrassing.

I had nothing to be embarrassed about.

It was the "I can't go back" of warning.

There was danger in going back. Although the obvious interpretation would be one that warned against going back to a life or environment that had led to the life-threatening disease and subsequent pulmonary emboli that had been part of my life a few weeks earlier, that was not the warning that I heard. Going back, indeed, would be a threat to my life, but not to my life as it *was*, rather to my life as it *could be*.

This was the last call: *Go back and you will lose your life as it could be.*

Nothing more, nothing about what to do next: What about promises? What about commitments? What about responsibilities? What about loyalty? And if none of those: What about prudence? Nothing. No more intuition, just "I can't go back." That was probably the strongest intuition that I had ever had in my life. If I followed it, my entire life would change.

I would not have chosen that intuition, but it may have saved my life. It did not tell me *why* I should not go back or to *what* I should not go back; it simply told me not to go back. I would have to discover the *whys* later; however, it was not too hard to figure out to *what* I should not go back. There were only two things going on in my life at that time: work and family. Of those two, there was no question in my mind of leaving my family—that was never going to happen—but I was not planning to leave my work either.

I remembered that the psychologist Erich Fromm says that productive work and loving others is a sign of individuation. Now the intuition was challenging me to go beyond work and/or love.

This was a high-stakes intuition.

The intuition had come at one of those unusual moments in life when powerful events eclipse one's normal life and make it possible to look at that normal life differently. The powerful events in my life at that time were a diagnosis of vulvar cancer and the surgical removal of that possible cancer accompanied by complications. The complications ranged from life-threatening to frustrating.

At the time of the surgery, I did not acknowledge the power of those attending events, although I was aware of their existence. I did not see the storm on the horizon. As captain of my ship I intended to sail through that experience, return to home port, and go about my usual life as a terrestrial being.

Instead, the complications following the surgery softened the boundaries of my world and made room for the entrance of the intuition. The intuition immediately became the directional rosette on my life map. It pointed north—only north—and said not to go back.

South was my life.

It took at least two months for the softening to occur, for the boundaries of my world to become pliable. Two more months passed as I tried to get rational control over uncomfortable emotions and to extract the message hidden within the events, and then another month elapsed as I wrestled with the decision to act. Five months, and that was not all: It took me some time after that to understand the enormous impact of my decision on my life and to fully incorporate the meaning of the experience into my being.

My usual approach to the world was cautious, analytical, and rational, the familiar characteristics of a college professor, especially a professor of philosophy, but looking back I can see that I did not have a chance either to ignore the intuition or to capture it in a rational web. This was to be a journey of consciousness and the intuition was to be my inspiration.

Along the way, I would lose my self-imposed title of "Captain of My Ship" and become once again "Humble Traveler" on the way to becoming a wiser and gentler person. My body and soul would travel on both adventurous water and solid, secure land.

The water included riptides.

Riptide

Life immediately after the surgeries and complications was like a riptide in which the incoming waves meet together obliquely and create an undertow that can pull a person from the shore and from safety. The surgical events and the intuition crashed together in my consciousness and together had the power to pull me under or to pull me out so far from the beach that I would not have the stamina to return. Either way I would drown. I was not willing for that to happen.

I had been raised near the beach in San Diego and had been cautioned to stay away from riptides. That was when I was younger and in prime physical condition; what would happen now if I should so engage? Ten years before the surgery, my sons had signed me up for a team half-triathlon in Santa Cruz. My cousin-in-law, Bob, did the run; my husband, Dave, did the bike ride; and I was assigned the swim around the Santa Cruz pier. My sons, Will and Ben, each did the complete half-triathlon on their own.

The younger and stronger swimmers started first. Dressed in my wet suit, I stood by as the life guards on their surfboards accompanied the first groups, one lifeguard light-heartedly pulling a large inflatable shark after his board. Santa Cruz had had its share of shark attacks. On the signal, I plunged into the very cold water, gasped to catch my breath, and began the swim around the pier. By the time I reached the end of the pier, head throbbing from the cold water, I was swimming on my back, counting in Japanese, and trying to ignore the huge sea lions that were sliding into the water 50 feet away from me. The life guards chatted with me to determine whether I had hypothermia like some of those who had already been pulled from the race. Rational conversation saved me then; I completed the race, though I ultimately came in last. Dave and Bob made up the lost time while I stood for a long time under a hot shower in order to stop the uncontrollable shaking of my body. Now, ten years later, symbolically, I felt the power of the ocean water again and turned to rational conversation to save me once more, this time without a life guard, this time talking only with myself.

In the months directly following the surgery and its accompanying intuition, throughout November and early December, I used all of my rational strength to gain control of the emotional and spiritual power of the experience. Compared to the emotional and spiritual pain at that time, the physical pain was minimal, not that my surgical wound did not hurt, rather that the wound in my soul had become so great that it made everything else, including the upcoming holidays, insignificant.

I knew that I had to gain control of the experience that I was going through for two important reasons: First, I had to make sense of the entire experience in my life in order to understand and overcome the powerful emotions that had followed it, and second, I had to discover what meaning this experience held for me so that I could deal with the message in the intuition—even if I considered my family ties to be sacrosanct and beyond the reach of the intuition, I, at least, had to make a decision about returning to my work at the college. Beyond those two reasons, I wanted to feel like myself again. To do that, I had to get rid of the powerful emotions and intuition involved, and I was intent on doing that quickly.

I immediately thought about Leibniz, the philosopher, who emphasizes our need to make sense of the world by seeking rational explanations for events. I strongly agreed that, for the most part, human beings both seek and assume causes and rational explanations. Even the coroner writes "causes unknown,' rather than "no cause" when he submits a report on a baffling death. I was not dying in body, not dead in soul, but I had been struck down in spirit and I needed to understand why. I needed a rational explanation for everything that I had gone through in the previous two or three months.

That, I optimistically assumed, would make all the pain and emotion go away.

Reason To The Rescue

More emotion was the last thing that I desired at that time, so I enthusiastically turned to reason for my support. I had every confidence in reason as the path to the resolution of my problem. I saw nothing unusual about analyzing either my emotions or my intuition rationally—nothing except the fact that reason by itself did not reduce the power of either one. In the long run, reason by itself became both the intuition's adversary and the co-conspirator of fear when it came time to act. Unbeknownst to me then, reason would need a partner.

I knew that I had just undergone a physical and emotional trauma the depth of which I had not anticipated. That trauma had been exacerbated by the fact that I had been wounded not only in body, but also in soul, and no one seemed to be paying attention to souls. The need for surgery had been accepted; the trauma to my soul had been completely unexpected.

I was not accustomed to being in such emotional situations, let alone succumbing to them, so I set about working my way beyond the trauma. I first sought help from the surgeon and the physician. Beyond their medical training that told them to keep their distance from patients, the surgeon could not give me any help because he was neither interested in nor able to understand what I was going through, and he was content to have my concerns fall beyond his job description; the physician, while giving me both empathy and some guidance, seemed to know that I was going to have to transcend the trauma by myself. The physician was right, as I would learn later: It was my trauma; it was my problem.

If that were the case, I would play to my strengths. I would solve the problem through reason. My plan was to find meaning in the entire surgical experience and then to use that meaning to rid myself of the emotions and the intuition that had followed the surgery. I would find the meaning in the experience by identifying those facets of the traumatic event that were most powerful for me. Once I had collected my set of images, I could determine—one-by-one—what they stood for symbolically, and then I could search for the manner in which those symbols were operating in my life. Drawn together, the symbols emerging from the experience and their application to my usual life might provide me with the personal insight, the "message," that would neutralize the uncomfortable emotions and shed light on that to which the intuition was telling me not to return.

The philosopher, Immanuel Kant, might have liked my approach. Kant argued that knowing is always relational, based on contributions from both the knower and the thing to be known. The facets that I chose for my approach were out there, somehow, in the experience and most observers would have noticed them.

Not everyone would agree that the symbols were in the experience as well; only those attuned to meanings would have noticed the symbols. The psychologist Carl Jung says we all have such symbols in our collective unconscious and respond to them whether we realize it or not.

The third step of the approach, the application of the symbols to my life, was my personal creative contribution to the process.

The meaning that I drew from the application of the symbols to my life was what I called "personal insight." I usually thought of personal insight as something intuitive and fast. In this story, however, the personal insight grew slowly due to my resistance to acknowledging trauma in the first place, and then to my resistance to making change.

My next step beyond creating the plan was to stonewall the entire project and hide out where I was most comfortable.

Circles Of Knowledge

Committed as I was to a rational explanation for the experience, there was a complication. The complication was that I had been professionally trained in philosophy and had spent many years within the discipline. I wrestled with the philosophic legitimacy of my approach to the problem in ways that probably would not have seemed important to others, but which were part of who I was. The wrestling was a significant component of my experience. It may have contributed to the strength upon which I drew to get myself out of the whole situation, but it also slowed down my search.

In the back of my mind, I knew that there are several ways of knowing. They were pictured in my mind as concentric circles, any one available to me according to my choice. That was nice to know, but I also knew that my choice was limited by my professional training. Not all of those circles were acceptable to my colleagues, the professional philosophers. Lurking in the back of my mind, along with those circles of knowing, was the awareness that I possibly could be drawn beyond the respectable circles in my search for a resolution to my problem.

I sorted through the embedded circles housed in my mind. The innermost circle was the smallest circle. It contained the fewest kinds of things that could be known. That was due to the fact that it had the most constraints for knowing; the more rules there are for knowing, the fewer are the kinds of things that can be known. In that first circle, only physical things could be known.

The next circle was larger and had different criteria, different rules, and that was true of all of the circles through at least those four levels. Each circle was bigger and more inclusive than the one before it because its criteria for knowing became fewer and often less rigorous, and so there was more that was considered to be knowable in the outer circles than in the inner circle, but also more to be worried about.

The rational explanation that I was seeking would be found in the second circle. That was the circle of knowledge from which I expected to transcend this experience. It would turn out that the second circle would not be enough by itself.

First-circle Sensory Knowledge

I knew that the explanation for my wounded soul would not be found in the innermost and smallest circle of knowing. The surgeon, my husband, and my oldest son, would disagree. I knew that was coming. The first circle represented empiricism, the approach used by scientists. Its rules require *physical* evidence for knowledge, an indirect *link* to physical evidence, or, if it were impossible to test the physical evidence at that stage, a statement of how one *would* proceed when circumstances for such a test became available.

An empirical explanation for my various traumas—physical, emotional, and spiritual—would require evidence that was not only physical and, therefore, measurable, but that was also available for others to experience in a repeatable way. In order to follow those rules, my post-surgical sadness and loneliness would need to be reduced to something physical, probably chemical, and their explanations would turn out to be nothing more than varying levels of whatever physical thing was being measured: no meanings, no growth, no purpose in the events, just subtle physical changes within the body.

The reduction of my sadness, for example, to chemistry or behavior assumes that we can know no sadness-in-itself, no emotion of sadness, merely chemical changes or tears. Once the sadness as a metaphysical entity or as an emotion is banished from the empiricist's world, the "why" of my sadness and any meanings or messages that I sought would have no place in their explanations.

Spiritual feelings would be the result of chemical/electrical change in the body as well. Using the empirical method, there can be no empirical knowledge of souls, of God, or of thought, because such entities are not material and therefore cannot be measured according to the rules of empiricism.

Even given my disagreement with an approach that defines as unknowable such immaterial entities as God, souls, and abstract values, I would have been the last person to question the value of empiricism for our lives as *one way* of knowing. Empiricism, with its strict rules for knowing, has provided the Western world with the spectacular growth in standard of living that has occurred within the last few centuries and has impressed us all within the last fifty years with an amazing array of incredible new technologies and biological discoveries.

This one way of knowing, this first-circle way of knowing, was not suitable for my plan to seek symbolic meaning in the physical, emotional, and intuitive experiences through which I had gone for another reason: Beyond my approach violating the rules of empiricism, it also violated the methodology of empiricism. Even if symbolism and meaning *were* assumed to exist, the additional existence of a connection between physical events and such symbolic concepts—if even entertained—would have to be tested empirically. The link itself would have to be testable. I would have needed to gather all kinds of data following some empirical design that would show that there was a tendency, say, for people who had similar physical ailments to have a similar set of emotional or spiritual concerns. People who had lung problems, for example, would need to be found to have some life situations that could be solved, or at least addressed, by symbolism related to air, breath, spirit, and other lung-related concepts. What would have begun for me as a search for meaning through symbolism would have evolved, in the first circle, into a search for empirical correlations. I did not know at the time that others already were addressing that issue, but I did know that such a search would neither have solved my problem nor have been of interest to me then.

As I mused about connections, I thought about the four causes that Aristotle identified: The "efficient cause" is the *event* or agent which brings the entity into being. My surgery would be the efficient cause of my sadness. The "material cause" is that of which the thing is made. In my case, the chemical changes in my body would be considered the material cause of my sadness. The "formal cause" is the nature or essence of the entity. The formal cause of my sadness would be found in the biological and psychological *structure* of the human organism and its interaction with the external world. The "final cause" is the *purpose* for the sadness . . . and that was what I was looking for.

The empiricist can talk easily of efficient and material causes—of surgeries and chemicals—and, in theoretical moments, of formal causes—of the biological make-up of the human being. I wanted to talk about purposes, meanings, and messages, about final causes.

The empiricist's circle was small in my visual model because its criteria for truth are so rigorous and because those criteria and the assumptions of the theory apply only to physical things. Small is not bad . . . unless one wants to find meaning in traumatic events.

Three of the major players in my life at the time of my surgery were committed, trained, and high-achieving empiricists. Their opinions really mattered to me. But I was headed outside that small circle.

Second-circle Rational Knowledge

I had great respect for first-circle empiricists and their approach, but I was not worried about going beyond them and their circle because the second circle, a little bit larger, also commands great respect in my professional discipline. The third and fourth circles are another story.

Rationalists, the inhabitants of the second circle, accept the criteria of the empiricists, but only as one way of knowing. Rationalists do not limit their knowing to physical things and so they inquire about God and souls and mental events. I was intellectually comfortable in that circle and was aware that symbolism is an acceptable topic in that circle.

The criteria for truth in the second circle are about the testing of *ideas*, not the measuring of *things*. The three most well known ways of testing ideas for truth are correspondence, coherence, and pragmatism. Correspondence tests how closely an idea matches the thing or event that it represents in the external world. Coherence tests how well a new idea fits with older accepted ideas. Pragmatism tests whether an idea actually works when one tries to apply it to the outside world.

Rationalists test ideas, rather than things, and to do so they rely on a set of rules for the connection of ideas. This set of rules is universal in the

Western world and it is called "deductive logic." As if to underscore the fact that both the first and second circles are governed by reason, the first-circle set of rules for testing things is called "inductive logic."

Rationalists rely solely on logic—deductive or inductive—rather than scientific experiment as their method for finding the truth. The rules of logic are quite clear, are used by every rational person in the Western world, and are required in Western philosophy.

Is one set of logical rules better than the other? I smiled as I remembered the many, but different, attempts to claim absolute truth that were given by 17th and 18th century philosophers from each of the first two circles. Both groups of thinkers knew that they would have to attach their sets of rules to some absolute knowledge in the universe if they were to claim that their rules led to absolute truth. Seeking that absolute truth, they set out to find the absolute knowledge that would serve as its base—they spent centuries looking for just that: some knowledge that was absolutely true.

The empiricists had to wrestle with the fact that empirical knowledge—knowledge that we take in through our sensory organs—is often mistaken by us: things at a distance look smaller than they really are; sticks look like they are bent when dipped in water; the person we run after in the airport is not really the person we thought he was after all. So, empiricists looked for some sense perception that we could have about which we could not be mistaken: like a headache. If you feel a headache you have one; if you do not feel it, you do not have it. You cannot be mistaken about having a headache! This is interesting and fun, but not too helpful if we are trying to connect with the external world, the world around us. There is nothing out there in the external world about which we cannot be perceptually mistaken.

The rationalists took a different approach, one that began with ideas rather than things or sense perception. Is there any idea that we have that is absolutely certain, true by its very definition? There are several: for example, the idea of a triangle must include three, and only three, angles, and—due not to our thinking, but to its very nature—the sum of those three angles always equals 180 degrees. Whether there is anyone there to observe triangles, whether there is anyone there to think about triangles, triangles always have 180 degrees.

Headaches and triangles and absolute truth are the stuff of philosophical thought. So are symbols and meanings. It seemed to me at the time that my search for a meaning to my recent and traumatic surgical experience would be in the context of the second-circle rationalists' thinking. I knew, however, that rationalists had been criticized for building elaborate and beautiful conceptual systems that are unrelated to the "real world,' the world that we live in daily. I certainly did not want my symbolic meanings to get that sort of label.

I also wondered at what seemed to be my pull at that time to the less rational third and fourth circles.

Third-circle Knowledge By Faith

The third concentric circle in my mind was characterized by faith rather than reason. The difference between faith and reason depends on whether one defines "faith" as a kind of thought or as an attitude. As a kind of thought, faith often is set between reason and opinion; reason has evidence or support for its truth, opinion does not. Faith as a kind of thought is like belief: the confident conviction that something is true, even without having empirical or rational support for its truth. That definition suggests that faith is like a weak or unsupported knowing, better than opinion which is acknowledged not to have support, but not as good as reason where the support is known. Furthermore, it is claimed that not only is there something missing in faith—namely evidence or support—but that there is something added. That added component is an act of will: the will to believe.

Why would anyone willfully believe in a statement that had little or no support?

Theologians have argued about that for centuries and their arguments often begin with St. Thomas' claim that the faith mentioned in the above definition is a propositional belief; that means that it is a *statement* about something and its attributes, for example, the statements that all triangles have three angles or that some apples are red. With a propositional belief, we fall back into the second circle where we test such statements with logic or the first circle where we test them with observation or experiments.

But not everyone thinks that faith is about statements: Centuries after St. Thomas, Martin Luther argued that faith is not a belief *that* something has an attribute, but a belief *in* something. Luther claimed that faith is based on an *attitude* of trust and commitment. Philosophers like Kierkegaard and William James agree. For Kierkegaard, belief in God is not securing proof of God's existence; belief in God is not a first or second circle activity. Belief in God requires a "leap of faith."

That is the whole idea: faith just is committing to and trusting in someone or something by choice. Faith is not just a weaker kind of reason, nor is it a special kind of perceptual observation or logic. The concept of faith does not have the dual function that the concept of belief has. Sometimes "belief" is used in connection with propositions and in that use means "weak reason," and sometimes "belief" is used in connection with emotion and in that use means "have trust in," but the concept of faith is only about trust and commitment; faith is other than reason altogether. It is a feeling, like love or trust, combined with a desire and a commitment.

Over two thousand years ago, Plato told us that the highest of all existents was "The Good" and that, whatever it was, it was higher than Existence, Knowledge, or Pleasure. Later, Christian mystics defined Plato's "Good" as God, although that would not have been appropriate in the early Greek philosophy. As rational as Plato was—and he *really was*, being the philosopher who posed most of the questions that we study today in philosophy, as well as providing us with answers that frame today's discussions—it is clear that, for him, gaining awareness of or contact with The Good is gaining awareness of or contact with something other than knowledge. The search for that connection—the search for wisdom—Plato told us, was like being in love.

Third circle faith is not a rational justification for any particular state of the world; rather it is a way of living in the world, a way of approaching the world. It involves trust and confidence in something (deism) or someone (theism) who is responsible for or equivalent with the order and progress of the world, believing *in* that someone or something, not believing *that* that someone or something exists.

There are *rational* arguments for the existence of God, but many of them seem to appeal to those who already have faith in God. Furthermore, for believers, trust in and commitment to the source, deistic or theistic, usually are not open to rational questioning, certainly not to empirical measurement and often not to Western logic. Science and logic simply do not apply to their belief in God, anymore than they apply to love.

Non-believers frequently challenge believers in ways that are unimportant to the believers: "Where is your proof?" they say, not realizing that there is no proof in love. "How could the God that you trust do that to you?" they ask, not yet recognizing that such a question does not count against the believer's faith in God since the trust is unassailable.

Individuals who have trust and confidence in such a spiritual someone or something—like God or the universe—also have personal approaches to life that are consistent with their level of trust and with their views of that spiritual source. Such an approach might incorporate, for example, an ethical code of behavior or the acceptance of underlying meanings of events that happen to us.

The individual who has faith in such a spiritual source often does not find a need to test his or her corresponding approach to life against empirical evidence or rational logic, because the approach follows from the source itself, and that source is accepted emotionally rather than rationally. What that individual does have to do is be very sure that there is *consistency* between his or her approach to life and the source on which that approach is based. Searching for that consistency *between* the spiritual source and the individual's approach to life *is* a rational activity and such a search is of paramount importance. There are many examples of people carrying out personal lives that are inconsistent with their descriptions of the source to which they are committed.

The fact that the acceptance of the source is *not* a rational activity does not mean that the acceptance of the source and its corresponding approach to individual life are based on rational error; merely that the support of the source is something other than reason. The acceptance is based on love.

Religious people often accept truth based on third-circle thought, testing truth for its compatibility and consistency with their faith in God. In fact, until the Middle Ages most people accepted truth according to faith rather than empirical evidence; most people operated within the third circle.

The ascendance of reason and the demotion of faith since the Middle Ages is a story well-chronicled: During the Middle Ages, reason, especially an empirical variation, worked its way up from being *unacceptable* as a source of knowledge at all, to becoming an *accepted but subordinate* source of knowledge to faith, then to becoming an *alternate and compatible* source of knowledge alongside faith, and finally to becoming the *preferred* source of knowledge in the Western world for the past several centuries.

Reason has come to be preferred on several counts: it has universal, public rules; it works *i.e.,* it leads to positive outcomes for many, many people; it allows individuals, among themselves, to transcend disparate beliefs about touchy issues; and, especially in the case of empiricism, it seeks understanding of the structure of the physical world in order to learn more about it, including the people in it. Reason also keeps passion (emotion) in check and protects us from the vagaries of appealing to ungrounded or even dangerous belief systems. In a world that contains many religions and a variety of faiths, it is imperative that the common language among religiously diverse peoples is the language of reason.

Though a trained philosopher and a devotee of reason, both empirical and rational, I approached the world with trust and commitment. I thought that there are life experiences that transcend rational explanation, at least at the current stage of human development. I believed that the big questions—like the meaning of life—require answers from each of us, even as we do not have all the information or knowledge that we would need to rationally answer those questions. In one sense, we all base our lives on faith of some kind: Some people have faith in science, others in reason, and still others in a transcendent source. Each of our lives is based upon some very basic assumptions and personal interpretations about the meaning of life: more or less conscious, more or less rational, more or less our own, more or less true, more or less useful, more or less positive, and more or less humane.

Because so much is at stake in our personal interpretations of life, both individually and globally, it was surprising to me how little attention we pay to those interpretations. Yet even as I thought that, in my search for the meaning of my current situation I was ignoring the force of my own interpretation of life, assuming it without question, and relying, instead, solely on reason—until the results of a rational analysis of my recent trauma pushed me right up against my own interpretation of life.

I did not know it then, but reason by itself was not going to remove either the emotional wounds of the surgery or the struggle with the intuition that I could not go back, whatever that might mean.

Fourth-circle Knowledge Through Personal Insight

I was vaguely aware that out beyond the faith-based circle, in circle four, is an approach sometimes collectively called "New Age" teaching. It includes parapsychology. Mysticism is there, too, unless it is systematic, in which case it would be in the third circle. Also in the fourth circle are fortune telling, astrology, divination, psychic knowledge, extrasensory perception, spiritual healing, intuition, and spiritualism—for starters.

Many of those means of seeking knowledge are very old and are precursors to systematized religion, in some cases absorbed into later religious doctrine. I suspected that the contemporary return of many of those approaches to knowledge—considered by many to be superstitions—might be a contemporary response to the reluctance of empiricism, the currently dominant system of knowledge, to consider how to incorporate non-physical experiences into its methodology.

As I explored that fourth circle, it appeared that it has no formal methodological umbrella. The individuals working in that fourth category seem to accept looser and fewer criteria for knowledge than those accepted in each of the other three circles. Each of the other three circles has limits beyond which the thinkers cannot go if they are to be consistent with the rules of their chosen methodology. The fourth circle does not appear to have such established limits. That is why it is so big, why it is filled with so many possibilities.

Empiricists have their physically-based criteria of measurability, objectivity, and replicability. Rationalists have their tests of coherence, correspondence, and pragmatism. Those who base their knowledge on faith have to be sure that their approaches are consistent with the way that they view the spiritual source. In the fourth circle are those who are not operating within such unified systems and who are not grounding their thoughts and writings in physical correlations, rationally connected ideas, or systematic religious faith, but on personal experience. Indeed, many of the inhabitants of that circle argue that the reliance on the mental actually is a problem when seeking truth. Often they struggle for words to explain what they have experienced. Some of their experiences are unusual within our common approaches to life; some are ineffable. In my literary excursion into the fourth circle I found myself not among the irrational, but among the non-rational. There was nothing wrong with that, but that was not where I had intended to be.

Predictably, the mystics and the psychics are in the fourth circle, but, less obviously, many contemporary and eclectic motivational speakers and writers are out there too—if they are not linked to a religious doctrine. Power of positive thinking belongs there. I found myself thinking that it is an intriguing circle, but that it also might be a dangerous one, dangerous because it has no set of truth-criteria that govern the entire circle. It could be more difficult to distinguish the wise from the opportunistic in that circle. It certainly is not a circle that shares the established and positive reputations of the other three circles.

The rather shaky reputation of the fourth circle could be due to its perceived newness, although many of the thoughts within it actually are very, very old. That shaky reputation also could be due to the fact that, lacking clear standards for truth, it draws the flaky, like the "breathologist" in Marin County, California who, while arguing that we can get all of our nutrients from the air, had a secret supply of junk food and junk food *wrappers* in his bureau drawer.

None of the fourth-circle information, beyond my awareness of its existence, crossed my mind in the middle of my experience . . . even as I started reading the literature of the fourth circle. I did not have to worry about any of that because I was not going there.

Which Circle?

As I settled into second-circle rationalism, I reminded myself that reason could be a game and that it could be used to avoid addressing important questions. I did not intend for my rational analysis to become a game. I might have thought of it as just an exercise at the beginning, one that could distract me from the power of the intuition or, better yet, one that I could use to improve my life, but I never thought of it as frivolous. Such analysis was something that I did well, it was respectable, and it was safe; hence, my self-assurance.

I was comfortable within the boundaries of rational thought, happy to stay within the second circle as I began to seek meaning in my experience. I began with a rational, albeit non-traditional, analysis of the most powerful facets, to me, of my recent experience. I identified eight images for analysis and named them accordingly: "the vulvectomy," "the pulmonary emboli," "the gurney scene," "the surgeon," "the intuition," "the sadness," "the loneliness," and "the abandonment."

I fully expected my rational analysis to provide me with meanings of those events in my life. I also expected the analysis to allay my emotions of sadness and loneliness and to provide me with a response to the intuition. Certainly the analysis would provide a directional template for focus in a traumatic time: I would focus on the positive rather than the negative significance of the experience.

I had spent my entire professional life dealing with abstract ideas. I assumed the existence of a transcendental world. I spent a lot of time there. I was a rational, intuitive being, and everything about me exuded that. I did not care much about the world of commerce or about material things. I had little interest in the practical aspects of everyday life; I managed them, in most cases quite well, but I simply did not care much for them. I loved ideas.

I strongly believed, along with some philosophers and psychologists, that ideas lead to action, that it is a lack of integrity to know something and not to act in accordance with that knowledge. The ideas motivated me. I sought to make my actions compatible with them. I was an idealist.

The intuition that had erupted weeks earlier had the force of knowledge. At the moment, however, safely ensconced in second-circle rationalism, it seemed unlikely that I would heed its warning and "not go back."

That lack of personal integrity was a problem for me.

Connections

Early in December, two months after my surgery, in my car on the way to "The City," I cautiously presented to Dave, my husband, my idea about using the locations of my physical concerns as two of the images that might teach me something about the experience. He, with his empirical assumptions, saw no connection between the site of a physical problem and any meaning it might have for one's life.

I, on the other hand, had been thinking about the meaning of the locations of my physical concerns—the vulvectomy and the pulmonary emboli—since mid-October. I knew that such a search for meaning would be quite controversial in many philosophic circles, but it was interesting to me. Even as it was interesting, I knew that, as a philosopher, I would have to be able to defend the direction that I was going.

It was clear to me that many, if not all, of the physical concerns that we all have are somehow related to the lives that we live. Whether these physical concerns actually have intrinsic symbolic meaning or we merely ascribe such meaning to them, their nature and location can serve as the genesis of questions about our lives. In truth, *anything* can generate questions about our lives.

I found myself thinking about the beauty of the Rorschach test and other projective tests. The idea is that the person who is describing the inkblot will project into that description his or her way of viewing the world, his or her concerns. The individual's concerns will be revealed in the descriptions of the inkblots and later correlated with descriptions given by members of groups who exhibit certain clusters of behavior. At the very least, it seemed to me, the nature and location of physical problems could work the same way as a projective test: "So, you had pulmonary emboli; what do you make of that?" Physical problems and locations would be an especially interesting tool because of the many possible combinations and variations of problems and locations, and because the physical problems actually belong to us individually in a way that the inkblots do not. I was not worried about the projective approach in general, because well-known psychologists, like Sigmund Freud and Carl Jung, had used the technique successfully.

It is also true that some of these connections between our physical problems and our lives are quite obvious and clearly are more than just projections: we drink a lot of alcohol and we increase our chances of getting liver disease; we smoke a lot and we make ourselves more vulnerable to lung cancer. But I knew that that kind of connection was too simple for my question, because those examples assumed a strictly physical causal relation: physical behavior to physical problem.

My question was not about a psychological causal relation either: psychological stimulus to psychological response. We all know that different people can have different emotional reactions to psychological stress: some cry, some shout, and some withdraw. We do not have any aversion to talking about that. But once again, that might be due to the similarities between cause and effect.

I wanted to know about a more difficult kind of situation: three people, for example, in the same psychologically stressful situation: One gets a migraine headache, the second contracts conjunctivitis, and the third has no physical response at all. Here is a case of a psychological stimulus and a physical response, no, a psychological stimulus and several different physical responses. Demeaning words from a boss or supervisor, for example, are not physical things, yet the responses from the employees are physical responses, and these responses often vary with the individual. Why does the first person get the migraine, rather than the conjunctivitis? Why does nothing physical happen to the third person in the same situation?

Given whatever my life circumstances were at the time, was there any meaning in my getting Paget's Extra-mammary disease rather than any other disease? Or no disease at all? Does the person *choose* the physical response? Most of us do not experience that, certainly at the conscious level. But a person might be able to *use* the kind and location of physical responses to learn something about him-or herself.

Would there be something I could learn about my conscious being from the location of my physical concerns? Could I extract some meaning from this life-disruptive experience by seeking the symbolic meaning of the physical location and kind of recent illness in my body?

I was convinced that there was insight awaiting me in the query about the symbolic meaning of the locations of my illnesses as well as of the physical and emotional events that I experienced that fall. My philosophical and psychological training, indeed my very nature, ensured that I would seek the meaning of the events. I was not willing to delay that search any longer.

In fact, I already had begun; I had considered the questions of knowing to my satisfaction. What had seemed like a nod to academic rigor, of course, might well have been resistance to psychological or spiritual growth, to moving forward.

I began my rational search for meaning with great enthusiasm. I had not yet received the important warning that my committed reliance on reason itself might be making me vulnerable. I did not suspect that reason could fail to allay my emotional feelings and provide answers to my life decisions. I rested for a while in the rational eye of the hurricane, oblivious to the emotional storm clouds surrounding me.

I wanted to return to my old self. The "old self" to which I wanted to return, however, already was different than the one with which I began.

DIAGNOSING

Images and Symbols

Following my rational, if non-traditional plan, I identified eight images in the surgical experience that hopefully would direct me toward the meaning of the event. The images varied in kind: two were physical, three were relational, one was an intuition—*THE* intuition—and two were emotional. I followed Carl Jung's approach to dream analysis in choosing those images: they were the ones most important to *me*.

The first image was related to the surgery, a partial vulvectomy, and to the disease that had led to the surgery. Paget's Extramammary Disease is a cancer that is found in the genital or anal regions of women, often older women. It gets the label "Extramammary" because the disease more frequently is found in a women's breast. When in the breast, Paget's Disease reveals itself as an angry red rash on the areola of the breast, a rash that itches intensely. Frequently, the cancer on the skin is connected to a malignant tumor within the breast. Paget's Disease is very dangerous. As a cancer in the genital area, the disease presents itself as the same red rash and the same excruciating itch that would be found on the breast. The good news is that the location of the rash does not lead as frequently to a malignant tumor. When the rash is removed from the vulvar area, taking various amounts of surrounding tissue with it, the surgery is called a "vulvectomy." The site of the diagnosed cancer and its surgery became the first of my images.

The second image was related to one of the complications following the surgery. The day after the surgery, the nurses discovered that my intake of oxygen was low. They suspected a pulmonary embolism, a blood clot to the lung. Sure enough, there was such an embolism, not just one but five of them. In some ways, the emboli were more dangerous than the surgery. The clot travels through the arteries from its source, in my case the leg, going through the heart and lodging in the lungs where it can block the oxygen. Pulmonary emboli can lead to instant death. The lungs and the emboli blocking the oxygen became my second image pointing to the underlying meaning of this experience in my life.

The third image was connected to an experience that I had while traveling from the pre-operation room to the operating room. While riding on the gurney that was pulled by my surgeon and pushed by the anesthesiologist, I observed a simple interchange between the surgeon and another hospital staff member. At the same time, I moved back from the gurney in my mind; backing away in my mind allowed me to consider the entire picture from an observer's point of view. The view in my mind's eye spoke strongly to me for some unknown reason and remained in my memory after the surgery. The strength of its presence suggested that it might be an important image guiding me to the meaning of the entire experience, not just a memory of a moment passed.

Image number four was inescapable. My surgeon, a charming and capable young man, played a dominant role in my experience. For a time during the experience he was one of the complications. Now it was time to figure out what the interaction with the surgeon had meant to me. Why had he become so influential in my life? Perhaps that, too, was a part of the meaning of the experience.

The next image, number five, was the intuition that I could not go back. Why it should have inserted itself at this time in my life was a mystery. Certainly, I would have had my rational guard down during this unusual period in my life, but the intuition did not seem to have anything other than that to do with the surgery. Possibly it was related to the time that I would need to be away from work, or the interruption of my normal life activities, yet that did not explain the urgency. The urgency of the intuition's message was as significant as the message itself. That urgency did not leave me a lot of time to prepare for its bidding.

The sixth and seventh images were of emotions. One of them, sadness, is accepted as a fairly common response to surgery. It sometimes is called secondary depression when it is called into being, temporarily, by the surgery itself. My sadness did not seem to be in response to the surgery, however, but in response to a spiritual circumstance. It had more of the characteristics of a spiritual depression than a physical depression, though how one would distinguish the two from the outside I did not know. I did know that the sadness was not with me all of the time, that it came and went on its own schedule. I also knew that my interaction with other people was as it always had been; perhaps those interactions were even intensified. The sadness did not ever intrude upon them. Obviously, it would be important to discover that about which I was sad.

The other emotion, loneliness, was the seventh image. This emotion is not mentioned as a common response to surgery, so I would not have to untangle it from that. It also was not new to me. Since I spent so much time in the transcendental world of thought and ideas, it was only natural that I would welcome the company of others on those journeys. Poetry shared is far richer than poetry read alone. Academics spend a lot of time alone with their books and ideas, as well as time in communion with others when they share their ideas in teaching. Ideas and people are at the top of my interest level. They are the two primary foci of my life. Now, I had just had an experience that commanded all of my attention and that drew me to the heights of human existence, and I was there all alone—reading poetry by myself.

Finally, the last image was the surgeon's abandonment of my case—of me. Number eight on the list of images was the disheartening experience of being left alone in the nest. The surgeon had flown away. There was no one there to gently push me out of the nest. Not only was I to fly by myself, I would have to launch myself. This was to be a solo flight in all respects. No one could do this for me or with me. No surgeon. No flock.

So there they were, the eight images that would point me toward the meaning of the experience. They were selected by their importance to me, by the power that they had to insert themselves into my life. There may have been more images, but those were the ones that I noticed. What did they mean?

THE PRIVATE PLACE
(CREATIVITY)

Clearly, the genital region signifies creativity. Just as clearly, the cancer threat symbolized something eating away, consuming, devouring that creativity. My homework was apparent: Where in my life was my creativity under attack? The homework was clear, but not easy. Those kinds of questions rarely are easy because they force us to look at the lives that we are living in a new and different way and, if we are committed to growth, they usually require us to alter those lives, to do something differently. Had I wanted to do that on my own, I would have done so already, so an undesired or feared change was likely to be lurking around the corner. It certainly was for me.

The symbolism of the pulmonary emboli, the blood clots to the lung, was not so obvious to me. There was an immediacy about them that did not attach to the potential cancer. The cancer might have taken a long time to do its work; the blood clots could have meant instant death. The death would come from the blocking of oxygen headed toward the brain. I was looking at something to do with air, which symbolically is the breath of life, the life spirit. According to the Genesis account, it is what distinguishes a mud form from a person. My very life as a human being, my spirit, was being blocked somehow. Plugged.

Whether I was doing that to myself, or was allowing someone or some environment to do that to me, *my creativity was being eaten away and my very life spirit was constricted,* both events leading to death if not remedied. The former meant a slow lingering death, the latter an instant death. Safely in the hands of a very competent surgeon, a pulmonologist from the medical clinic, and a primary care physician who had the wisdom of two worlds, my next step was to apply my newfound insights to my daily life and to my being.

I was in no hurry to do that.

So far, with the news that the Paget's Extra-mammary Disease was not cancerous and that the emboli were treatable, I was happy to let that remain an intellectual exercise. Of course, as merely an intellectual exercise, there would be no psychological growth resulting from that line of thinking. Not until I actually discovered what was consuming my creativity and why my life spirit was plugged, would I make any progress. I simply was not motivated to do that in mid-October.

My motivation returned by surprise early in November. I had been on a reading jag since early October, one that would last for the following year. I read all kinds of books. I consumed them. The tape of my November 8th meeting with a spiritualist reveals that he mentioned a few authors in the field of spirituality; one of them was Caroline Myss. On November 10th, two days later, Penny, my sister-in-law, coincidently arrived with Caroline Myss' book *Anatomy of the Spirit* in her travel bag. I was no stranger to Jung's concept of synchronicity, a relationship that he considered to be an alternative to empirical causality. I could take a hint. I read the Myss book immediately.

I found that Caroline Myss had done for all illnesses what I had done with the vulvectomy and the pulmonary emboli, and that she had creatively fashioned a context for the connection between illness and symbol. By assuming the interaction of mind and body, and by drawing a correspondence between the Hebrew Tree of Life, the Hindu chakras, and the Christian sacraments, she had provided a foundation for the symbolic interpretation not only of the physical location of the chakras, but for the sorts of physical ailments that occur in each physical location. She had created a taxonomy of anatomical, physical, emotional, and spiritual connections.

I assumed, once again along Jungian lines, that the reader would know or discover which of the several possible connections in Myss' taxonomy were relevant to his or her life. For example, though a vulvectomy would seem to have something to do with sex, my focus had been on its connection to creativity. Before even starting to read Myss' book, I took a look at the chart she used to lay out the taxonomy. There in the row labeled "second chakra," I found, among other physical dysfunctions, ob/gyn problems. In the same row, I found among the emotional issues, issues of money, power, sex, and *creativity*. Bingo!

That would not have been as significant to me in the weeks prior to the intuition, nor would I have associated money and power with the genital regions of my body, as old as those associations are historically. Whatever my intuition was warning me about, money and power apparently were involved along with creativity. At that time, I would not have been an enthusiastic donor of either my money or my power to the cause of my human development! In fact, it was worse than that: at that time, both money and its corresponding power were insurance that I could live the life that I wanted to live. There was no way, *absolutely no way* that I was going to give up either money or power. I was happier thinking about creativity.

I quickly turned the page to find the fourth chakra, the one related to the lungs and the circulatory system. I did not find pulmonary emboli in the physical dysfunctions category but I did find lung cancer and I figured that was close enough. And there in the emotional issues category along with self-centeredness, anger, forgiveness, compassion, and grief, were, of all things, *trust*, *love*, and *loneliness*!

Caroline Myss' book and I spent a good number of hours at Starbucks every day. The Starbucks moments became a pleasant part of my healing routine over the months to come. That was interesting since I was not much of a coffee drinker. I was really there for the human community.

I soon knew all of the employees by name and they knew my name and what I ordered. Occasionally my latte was waiting for me when I arrived.

I spent a lot of time at Starbucks and at home thinking about the issue of creativity that had appeared in both my and Myss' symbolism of the genital wound. For twenty-three years I had valued the creativity of my work at the college. I loved to create courses, to choreograph them, and then to deliver them. I was a curriculum specialist as well. I had a quick eye for potential connections and could rapidly create and design innovative programs. I had been the founding chairperson of three academic departments at the college and the primary designer of each of their academic programs. At one time, I had been instrumental in the restructuring of the entire department of Academic Affairs, as well as in redesigning the Liberal Arts Program. During my last four years at the college I had created what may have been the most innovative international exchange program in the country. I had been responsible for creating a cooperative international degree that, should it come into being, would be the first of its kind in the world. I had not been lacking creative opportunities.

What did all that have to do with a vulvectomy? I had had the incredibly good fortune of having been assigned creative and meaningful work in the world. I had been blessed with creative opportunities at the college and before that in other kinds of teaching experiences. That made it a problem for me to figure out the symbolism of the vulvectomy. Where was my creativity being eaten away?

I came across an interesting passage in one of Carolyn Myss' books. She pointed out that just as the creation of a child could end in an abortion, so other kinds of creation could end that way as well. Creative work that does not come to fruition, that is not actualized, is much like an aborted child.

Within hours of reading that passage, I inadvertently tuned into the television history channel, a favorite of my husband's, but not one I would have selected on my own. The documentary was about the creation of a Soviet military ship that could fly a few feet above the water at very high speeds. Apparently that was a revolutionary idea and the government of the USSR at the time supported the development of the prototype as well as the creator of the idea. The political winds changed; a new leader came into power, and the project was reduced in prominence. The creator found himself working on his own project for someone who had been his underling until, eventually, interest in the project dissipated to the point where there was no longer a place for the creator at the research center at all. According to his daughter, he went home in despair and depression and died a short time later. The commentator concluded by stating that the ship had been a project ahead of its time, one that military personnel still considered interesting.

I was not a military history buff, but that documentary caught my attention for another reason. The Russian man was an individual whose creative idea was aborted by others. Myss had indicated that there were some environments in which abortions of creative ideas were commonplace. That gave me a new way of looking at the wonderfully creative years that I had spent at the college.

There was no question that the college had given me creative opportunity; there was no question that my work was creative; there was no question that my life at the college had enhanced the college. There also was no question that many of my ideas were ahead of their time at the college. All of that was positive, but there also were shadows at the college that threatened my creativity. I usually did not dwell on the negative, it was not my approach to life, but when I did, it did not take long to find those external threats to my creativity and to acknowledge the immense energy that I occasionally had had to use to save "the baby."

It was only after I read Carolyn Myss' comments about the negative power of aborted creations that I began to understand that my many creative contributions to the college also included those creations that never came into being or those whose birth I had had to defend and protect with my own personal energy. The very environment in which I worked included a few individual, but serious, threats to my creativity. That was the message of the vulvectomy.

What was the message of the blood clots?

The Breath Of Life
(Spirituality)

I had not yet rationally figured out in my mind how my spirit was plugged. It became clear to me in the ensuing weeks that though the college and I were on compatible missions, we were not on the same mission.

The college sought a strong, narrowly defined, possibly innovative, international center that would support the college's *existing* role in international education and acknowledge the college's full-time resident international students. I sought a new level of international dialogue, one in which we listened to each country's cultural concerns and acknowledged that each country's concerns were of equal importance to those countries expressing them—an international dialogue in which we sought some common cultural thought on which to base our very different approaches to life, something akin to the foundational truths that the philosophers of the 17th and 18th centuries had sought.

The college wanted to include international education as part of its traditional curriculum. I wanted to introduce innovative international education throughout the world in the service of moving humanity forward. Our missions were clearly different, though related. Theirs was an educational mission that involved spirit; mine was a spiritual mission that involved education.

There was nothing wrong with the college mission or with my mission. We were just growing in different directions. At this time in my life, I needed to be working with or creating an organization that understood and supported my mission. I needed a place to work where my spirit could be free and unplugged.

As I acknowledged an environment that, on occasion, had challenged and been slow to value my creativity, and as I recognized a subtle, but critical difference between the college's mission and my own, I was coming closer to addressing the question underlying the intuition: *What was it to which I could not go back?*

It began to appear that I needed to move forward from the college. At the same time, I knew it was important to note that I was not going *away* from the college . . . I was going *toward* something new.

The View From A Gurney
(Reason And Emotion)

Beyond my project to discover the symbolism related to the locations of my health concerns, I decided to tackle the symbolism of the image I called "the gurney scene." Perhaps, I thought, I could make some sense of it, too. I was eager to do that because it seemed that the powerful effect of this image on me was an intriguing part of the entire process of growth. I was drawn to this image also because I thought that it was going to be easy to understand. I knew how to deal with it, and I assumed that it was going to go in a direction with which I was comfortable.

Here we go again.

My first look at the symbolism of the gurney scene occurred right after the second surgical procedure. I did not then have any inkling that the experience was going to be far deeper than I ever could have anticipated, that it was not an intellectual exercise, and that I definitely was not in control of the manner in which it played out, not in control of the process. At that time, my analysis was primarily an intellectual distraction from the physical events through which I was going. I turned to the depth psychologists for my rational analysis of the gurney scene.

Probably the most famous psychologist of the twentieth century was Sigmund Freud. I knew that his theory would support my search, both in the theory's introduction of the unconscious and in the extent to which it had embedded itself in Western culture: Research, art, music, literature, drama, counseling, the very language of the common person on the street, all resonate with Freudian vocabulary, Freudian ideas. But as easy as it would have been to turn to Freud's theory, I went instead to the ideas of Carl Jung.

Carl Jung, a medical doctor like Freud, was the heir apparent to the Freudian system. Jung and Freud had had a very close, almost father-son, relationship. When it ended, they never spoke with each other again. The source of the break was their disagreement about the motivational energy of the human being. Freud believed that all the causes of human personality come from behind, from the past; personality is *pushed* from the past. Jung had agreed with the idea of pushes from the past, but had thought that there also are *pulls* from the future, an idea that Freud could not accept. Pulls from the future were too closely linked with the idea of God or with spiritual life, concepts that Freud intentionally had excluded from his system. If pulls existed, though, as Jung thought, they could be used to guide us toward more fulfilling lives. That was the guidance for which I was looking.

Both Freud's and Jung's systems were early attempts to clarify the non-physical world, the world of consciousness, to provide it with a language and a system, which was exactly what I needed. It was in Jung's system that the gurney scene belonged. The moment in time, which I so vividly remembered, included the surgeon pulling the gurney, with me on it, and the anesthesiologist pushing the gurney from behind. Pulling and pushing both working together—Jungian theory was perfect for that.

In the gurney scene, the surgeon already had distanced himself from me, but was going to protect me against danger. The anesthesiologist had promised to be my safety net. I, the person on the gurney, was in danger, but I was going to be okay. I would note later that I, the person on the gurney, had no control over the events that were about to take place and was completely comfortable with that. I would learn more about that later when my personal archetypes unexpectedly became part of my rational analysis.

Who were those people in the scene; what did they actually represent? Although the woman on the gurney was also the narrator, Jungian analysis placed them all inside me. The scene was not about the surgeon, the anesthesiologist, and me. Those three individuals were symbolic, each representing a part of my unconscious, and they were clues to what was in there. Those clues, if recognized by me, would help me to develop my conscious being, help me to discover my journey.

On the day of the second surgery, the surgeon had pulled my gurney along the middle of the hospital corridor, commanding the space as his own. As another gurney approached from the opposite direction, the anesthesiologist told the surgeon that the custom in the hospital was to move on the right-hand side. The surgeon immediately corrected course, let the other gurney pass, and then swung my gurney into an operating room on the left. I lay on the gurney the entire time, observing, trusting, and non-involved. My mind observed the entire scene from some objective point.

I took the surgeon, who clearly was the most significant player in that scenario, to be my masculine side, the patient to be my feminine side, and the anesthesiologist to represent my personal unconscious. I toyed with the idea that the anesthesiologist was my shadow, the negative side of my ego, but although, as an anesthesiologist, he certainly was a shadowy figure in the scene, there was nothing negative about him or about his assurance that he would support me. Instead, he represented the shadowy world of the unconscious in which I felt safe.

The facet of the masculine/feminine dichotomy that was most important to me was the rational/emotional dualism. Once again, Jungian analysis, as opposed to Freudian analysis, allowed the individual's choice and interpretation of important images. With that in mind, the gurney scene represented to me a very active, capable, protective rational aspect of my personality that was working independently (the surgeon); a passive, trusting and apparently vulnerable emotional side (the patient); and an unconscious (the anesthesiologist) that was extremely supportive of my emotional side and was prepared to speak out and give guidance to my rational side: Reason and the unconscious working together, reason pulling, the unconscious pushing. I was aware that the rational side had acknowledged and responded to the guidance of the unconscious without missing a beat.

That was a lot of power applied to the support of that endangered emotional side of the psyche symbolically lying on the gurney. Could this be a scene about the future? Could it be that negative emotions were about to arrive, ones which I had to be certain to remove from my being? Was I at risk of having the promise of my new level of life threatened by negative emotions?

Even as I, unknowingly then, was about to be confronted by the unanticipated negative emotions of sadness and loneliness, I found myself happy to leave the rational analysis there. Except for the idea of endangered emotions, there was nothing compelling in the symbolism. I had other things to do and no particular motive to explore the image of the gurney scene any further. At the moment, there was no energy attached to that exercise, for that was all it was to me at the time. Even with such a clear warning, unheeded, my emotions remained unprotected—unprotected from the surgical experience, unprotected from the surgeon.

The Surgeon
(Passionate Intensity)

Enter the surgeon. And the energy. There clearly was an energy connection between the surgeon and me, even from the first day. He may have had that connection with all of his patients. I did not know and it did not matter. It was energizing. It gave me a sense of well-being as I entered into the procedures of the first five weeks. The energy was serendipitous. Had the surgeon been one of the non-communicative surgeons, I still would have entered the experience with trust and confidence, and probably with no fear, but the energy would have been missing. Trust and confidence had characterized the small number of other surgical procedures that I had had in my life. Never before had the personality of the surgeon been significant. This time was different.

The energy was pleasant and occasional. It did not matter to me when the surgeon arrived or how long he stayed on his hospital rounds. I did not think about him when he was gone because I knew he was coming back. He was like an old friend.

That did not last long. At the end of the first post-operative visit, he casually had said "come back in three weeks, but don't come running back before then." The comment had a sting to it, especially since I was not the running-back type. That was not the way old friends treated each other. By the time of the second surgery, two office visits later, the surgeon had completely withdrawn, and I was hurt and angry.

I knew what to do with the energy connection, but it was not clear where the hurt and anger came from. That knowledge came later. As for the energy, I had learned from Jung what to do in those occasional moments when energy connects intensely. The connection was clearly an animus attraction. That meant that I was strongly pulled to the energy of the surgeon because he had some qualities that I was lacking. It would have been easy to mistake the intense energy of an animus attraction for a romantic attraction. I knew that many people had made that mistake. This clearly was not a romantic attraction, but it was an inescapable and strong attraction. What did he have to teach me? What did he have in his life that was missing in mine? The answer came from the gurney scene.

Earlier in the analysis, I had thought of the surgeon as confident, competent, charismatic, skilled, and filled with energy. When I thought back on the gurney scene a week later, I found myself feeling *envious* of the surgeon. Where did *that* come from? I had many of the same characteristics that he had. In many ways, watching him was like looking into a mirror. Animus attractions, however, are for something missing, not something shared. What could it have been that I was missing?

Not professional degrees. Our degrees were equivalent; he had an MD; I had a PhD. Both degrees were from well-known and respected universities.

Maybe the difference had to do with status. He worked at a center connected to a world-renowned university research hospital and he was an up-and-comer. I taught at a small college down the street, and, though in a major position there, had a clearly blocked career ladder.

Maybe the difference had to do with a positive energetic environment. Everything appeared positive at that famous hospital, at least from a patient's perspective, and the surgeon was a member of the most highly respected group. I, too, was among the most highly respected group in my work environment and that extended even to China and my associations there, but the institutional environment was radically different in our two different places of work: the world-class success of the university filled its associates, employees, and patients with a confidence not found in a small college. The surgeon was in a positive, creative, energetic environment and he was having a more exhilarating experience than I was having!

Maybe the difference had to do with having a future. He, in his early forties, was in the competitive growth period of his career. I, in my early sixties, was in the synthesizing and mentoring period of my career. I loved working. Did I envy his timing in life? Was that what I had to learn?

I had made different life choices than he had made. I had chosen to marry twenty years earlier in life than he had. I had made choices that he would never have to make, like staying at home and raising my own children personally. Was there anything there?

Maybe it was the choice of career itself. While the prestige of our two very different professions was similar, I, on the one hand, had chosen to engage in work that had little financial reward, but immense *personal* reward in relation to other people; he, on the other hand, had chosen work that allowed him to avoid personal interaction but that was *lucrative* and had *ego* rewards in relation to skill and achievement.

At first blush, it seemed obvious that it was too late to change any of my choices or circumstances. Nor would I have wanted to in the case of my children and my students. Was the message, however, that <u>it was *not* too late to make changes?</u> Was the message that I still could choose, that there was work for me that would allow me to passionately use my creative energy in support of a spiritual mission?

This was more than an intellectual exercise.

The surgeon's energy, combined with the physical shock of the genital surgery, had awakened within me new levels of my own natural energy at the very same time that the same surgeon and the same surgery were sapping my existing energy. It became almost impossible to separate the surgery from the surgeon, the symbolism of the gurney scene from the symbolism of the surgeon, the positive from the negative.

From one perspective, the gurney scene and my interactions with the surgeon made clear to me that I needed to find a place where I could release my natural passionate intensity in my work. The message of the gurney scene was discouraging, though, because at that time the likelihood of my leaving my established profession and my beloved institution to create or join in something new was almost nil. I also was beginning to sense, but not yet understand, that I needed to protect my emotions from the surgeon himself.

From another perspective, the gurney scene and the surgeon became prominent images because they had energy in them. Together, they told me that it was time to grow, what to look for in the future, and how to prepare for dangers along the way. "Live with passion!" the surgeon's life had modeled. "Use reason to eradicate any negative emotions that attempt to come with you on the journey," the gurney scene had suggested. And there those negative emotions were, waiting for me in the shadows: sadness and loneliness. I soon would need to face them head on.

The gurney scene and the surgeon, together, provided a synergy that led me to question my work in the world. Looking back later, I could find the quiet voice of the unconscious guiding reason. Earlier, way back in the spring before the diagnosis and the ensuing surgery, before the beginning of this journey, I had recognized my feeling that I should back away from what I was doing. Managing the international program, rather than creating it as I had done earlier, was impinging upon more creative work. I had had no idea, however, how significant that feeling was until I came face to face with someone who was working with the passionate intensity with which I approached life. Now it was one year later and I was finally realizing how important the ephemeral feeling had been; I was finally listening.

But listening is not the same as accepting. Accepting entails acting and I had no intention of doing anything about all of that. There are a lot of people (most?) who are not living at their optimal level, who are not living out their destinies.

"Deal with it," I thought, *"What makes me so special?"*

Nothing, except that I knew better than to think that way; I knew what life could be like. I'd always known that.

I was no more special than anyone else.

I also was not living the optimal human life.

The Intuition (Destiny)

"I can't go back!"

If the vulvectomy and the blood clots had told me what was less than optimal in my life; if the surgeon had reawakened my natural energy; if the gurney scene had warned me to protect my emotions, to excise the negative emotions that were about to come, then the intuition had burned my bridges. I knew I could not go back!

The intuition had come in mid-October, just after the second surgery, joined forces with my energy pull to the surgeon, and intensified my desire to rationally clarify the gurney symbolism and the sites of my health concerns. Instead of telling me where to go beyond my present life, the intuition forcefully shoved me headfirst into my resistance to going at all. It made me address all of my newly identified worldly attachments that were revealed by the symbols: money, status, power, passionate intensity, and love.

The attachments were less about what I had and did not want to lose, and more about what I still wanted to attain. I had more money, status, power, passionate intensity, and love than most women in the world, than many women in the United States, but the comparison was irrelevant to me; the current situation was not what I had anticipated. It was not at the level that I desired. It was not enough. And the intuition that followed the second surgery had made that abundantly clear.

I had gone into the second surgery waved off by an empirical husband, a supportive anesthesiologist, an annoyed, withdrawn surgeon, and an angry wound that refused to heal until I paid attention. The symbolism of the gurney scene on the way to the operating room foreshadowed the level of life that was to come next. The anesthesiologist's claim that he was my life support system was the voice of my unconscious telling me that everything would be fine, that I would be okay on this spiritual journey.

With my last memory before that surgery being of the surgeon who had abandoned me before metamorphosing into the problem-solving craftsman, I left the world of reason, emotion, and intuition, and reluctantly awoke in the recovery room to a jarring reality. Dave arrived and delivered the seemingly good news that half of the endangered vulvar graft had remained and that the other half had little islands of successful graft that were likely to grow together. The surgeon, Dave reported, considered that to be a big success and Dave was visibly relieved and happy in his belief that this soon would be over.

Even as Dave spoke, the intuition erupted from whatever realm intuitions inhabit: *"I can't go back!"* I could not have accurately described that as a series of intuitions or even as a growing intuition; "eruption" was the appropriate word for that single intuition, both in a temporal sense and with regard to power. Think volcano! The intuition was there all at once and it was in all of me. It was different from the physical spasms of sadness or the mud-like loneliness that was to pour over my physical body a week later. It was clear, strong, powerful, concise, internal, compelling, and frightening.

There were only two things that were candidates for that to which I could not go back: my professional life and my family life. I had no other life at the moment, no active physical or social life, no emotional input from the arts and culture, no esthetic release, no separate spiritual life, no rest. I was far too busy at the college for those. I did not even have my beloved dog, Dizzy, anymore.

I could not go back; that I knew at some level, but not going back to work meant that I would have to give up money and its corresponding independence, title and status with their power for creative and meaningful contribution, the energy of my current life and work, and the application of my talents to a worthy cause; or, if I gave up family, I would have to give up all levels and kinds of love and commitment beginning with my immediate family, Dave, Will, and Ben, and extending to my brother, my bothers- and sisters-in-law, my cousins, my nieces and nephews, and Dave's mom and dad. The cat, the bird, the deck, the house, and the memories would go as well.

Run, hide, or fight? Which would it be? I chose to fight. Though I kept to myself what was going on internally until my struggle to make sense of it all became so painful that I had to tell my most trusted family and friends and tried to tell the surgeon, I, myself, did not hide from the intuition. Nor did I run. Throughout the experience, I had been as open and honest with myself as I consciously could have been, and I had done whatever I could to understand the significance of the intuition and the events of that fall.

I also fought that intuition with every means that I had. When I returned to the college a few months later, in mid-January, I had long since made my peace with the physical diagnosis and the surgery, even with the surgeon and the associated challenge to grow. My return to the college defied the intuition.

It was only the sadness and the loneliness that I could not seem to check.

The Sadness
(Disappointment)

I agonized over the intuition that followed my second surgical procedure in mid-October. The internal struggle was directly related to the sadness that was emerging, although I did not know that at the time. I did not understand it then, but the sadness was connected to my suspicion that I would not have the courage to follow the command of the intuition. I really did not think, then, that I would follow the intuition, yet the intuition was so strong that it could not be discounted. That certainly looked like a lose-lose situation for me. The price of living "the life that could be" was too high, yet if I did not listen to the intuition, I would know forever that I had turned my back on my personal destiny, on whatever it was for which I was here. After holding myself together for a week with that knowledge, not as clearly understood at that time, I was discharged from the hospital for a second time and went home to both physical and emotional sadness, my unconscious response to the personal price of fighting the intuition so intensely, of rejecting "the life that could be."

If, at that time, consciously, I had decided to accept the intuition and to give up either my professional life or my personal life, I could have more readily understood the advent of the sadness. I had been a teacher for a long time. I probably was born to be a teacher. I also had been a wife and a mom for a long time as well and that had been my most meaningful work in the world. It would not have been surprising to have had an emotional response of sadness if I had to leave any of that behind. But I was *not* leaving any of that! I had *not* accepted the intuition; I was energetically engaged in trying to make sense of it in order *to make it go away*; in order to get control of my life again.

Maybe the sadness had nothing to do with what I might have to give up. Maybe, instead, it had to do with the surgeon. The deep sense of sadness seemed to be intensified by the abrupt withdrawal of the surgeon. Not only had he taken back the energy that I was borrowing from him, he had taken back the partnership. It would have been easy to think that the sadness was due to the loss of my partner, the surgeon. I considered that, but it did not make any sense; the sadness was much too strong for that explanation. As for the loss of an external energy source, if I had known in advance that I was to go it alone I would have been all right, although I would have approached the experience differently.

No, the sadness was neither the result of the sacrifices that it seemed that I was being asked to make nor the loss of the energy or partnership of the surgeon. At some level I knew that I was in communication with something else and at a much deeper level. Maybe, and I thought about this with respect to the cancer diagnosis, maybe I was being made ready to die, to leave life as we know it, and maybe I was sad about that. That did not seem to be it either.

It was more as if I were sad about the way that I was living life, a life, by the way, that was not likely to have been considered undesirable by most people's standards. I settled on the belief that I was not being made ready to die, but being made ready to live at an entirely different level than I had been living before.

The problem was that I suspected that I was not going to follow the intuition. I knew that and, after teaching the "Hero's Journey" for a decade to scores of beloved students, there was a distinct sadness in recognizing that I was refusing the journey when its call came to me, that I was not a hero. How sad, how very sad, to knowingly refuse what Joseph Campbell described as "the call to adventure."

I tried twice to tell the surgeon what I was feeling. The second time, at the end of December, he listened. After that appointment, both the surgeon and I were busy. I was writing him a cover letter to the manuscript for the book about doctor/patient relationships, thanking him for the opportunity he had given me to talk; he was calling my physician to tell her that he was worried about me. Both of us were deadly serious about my response to the events surrounding my surgery. Befitting the different patterns of our beliefs and of our work in the world, I was going to address my emotions with thought; he was going to address them with chemicals.

I did not know about his phone call to my physician until later. Even without that knowledge, I decided not to send either the cover letter or the manuscript. I had wanted him to be the first to read the manuscript, but I was sensitive to the boundaries that might exist and so I did not offer it to him then, knowing that I would never tell the story without his reading it, that I would put it away in a drawer if he objected to it.

In the unsent letter, responding to his recommendation that I remove my sadness chemically, I made a reference to the distinction between viewing such experiences as I was going through as problems to be eradicated (his view) *versus* lives to be lived (my view). There is a huge difference between making emotions go away and learning why they came in the first place.

A few months later I began to wonder about that distinction and about my choice to directly face the post-surgical emotions in order to learn more about the experience and more about my life. Would I do it that way again? Had I been fooling around with something dangerous? Was life safer if it was strictly under empirical control? Would I have been better off to have matter-of-factly accepted my illness and surgery as a meaningless physical experience—as I originally had set out to do—passed by it as quickly as possible, and returned to my usual life?

Would I have been better off as an empiricist like Dave, Will, and the surgeon?

"Having second thoughts, am I, about my world view? Getting cold feet after that experience? Rethinking my commitment to rationalism? Getting a little nervous about the spiritual world? After all, it is one thing to lecture about Plato's transcendent forms and another to talk about having a commanding intuition. What is the difference between spiritual enlightenment and an ungrounded intuition? Have I been in any danger? I never felt that I was, but then again, I made the surgeon nervous. I was not afraid; should I have been?"

I had trusted the surgeon completely and he had suggested that I should simply get a prescription for some pills that would make my emotional discomfort go away. Characteristically, rather than supporting me in my approach to healing, he sent me off in his chosen direction and discounted my journey. His suggestion generated intense philosophical discussion among my family members and me about whether the taking of such mood-controlling pills abrogated the belief that emotions carry messages about life. Dave, Will, and Ben, each for different reasons, said that taking the pills to alleviate the sadness did not contradict the belief in the usefulness of emotions for psychological development. I disagreed. There was no way that I was going to take any chemicals to get rid of the emotions, for those emotions were telling me something about my life.

There is a beautiful scene in Hesse's *Siddhartha*, a story about one man's individual journey to enlightenment. Siddhartha spends his youth in spiritual study and searching. Along his way, he comes across Gotama Buddha and decides that part of the Buddha's enlightenment is based on the fact that the Buddha found this enlightenment through himself, not through the teaching of others. Siddhartha does not have enough worldly experience to do that, so he enters the world of commerce and love, joyfully at first, but then more and more as a spectator, a handsome, successful, wealthy, charming spectator, a spectator who has lost his way.

At about forty, he realizes that he is no longer on his path and he simply walks away from everything. He finds himself on the banks of a river that he had crossed as he entered the town within which he had learned about practical life. At the side of the river, he is so despondent about the loss of his self and his path, that he considers drowning himself in the very same river that will turn out to reveal the secrets of life to him later, unbeknownst to him then, of course. He is on the verge of falling into the river, when he hears his inner voice intoning the sacred, meditative sound, Om. He pulls back from the river and, exhausted, falls into a deep sleep under a tree.

When he awakens, he finds that an old friend from the past has guarded him throughout his sleep. They part company again, Siddhartha becoming a boatman on the river and learning from the river about the mystical union of all life. Finally, at the end of the tale, the friend, a seeker in his own right, but one who is searching for answers from others, meets Siddhartha again, this time when Siddhartha is the boatman. The friend recognizes that Siddhartha shares the same spiritual enlightenment that Buddha has; Siddhartha has become a Buddha himself.

My question to the surgeon would be this: If Siddhartha had been your patient, would you have prescribed mood-altering drugs to him when he struggled with the meaning of his life?

I was careful to note in my conversations with others that I was not trained in the use of chemicals for psychological or psychiatric purposes. I did not want to convey the idea that it was never appropriate to take medication for emotional concerns. I was not a medical expert, but it seemed clear to me that the source of the emotions was quite relevant to the decision. I understood that there are chemical changes and malfunctions in the body that can lead to emotional states that can be controlled best by chemical therapy. I was aware that tragedies can occur when the emotional state of an individual is not recognized and no help is given. It also seemed clear that the power and controllability of the emotions matters as well. When there is any chance that the individual might hurt him- or herself or others, or when that individual is unable to function according to normal social expectations, it seems that interventions might be appropriate. Who decides that is an interesting philosophical question to be left for another time.

I also was careful to note, in this highly empirical society, the dangers of dismissing the emotional and spiritual life by treating all emotional and spiritual experiences as if they are something to get rid of as quickly as possible, rather than seeing them as catalysts for enhanced human growth and development. I thought that it would be important, especially for the medical profession, to be able to distinguish between clinical depression and spiritual depression as Carolyn Myss does in *Sacred Contracts,* as well as to distinguish among physical, emotional, and spiritual concerns. It is time to acknowledge that although medical professionals are committed to the care of the body, the body is not the whole of the person. To disparage the emotional and the spiritual is to diminish important aspects of the person. The body, the mind, the emotions, and the spirit of the individual are closely connected. To tamper with one without considering the effect of that one on the others is to court disaster for the person; at the very least, there is the strong possibility that such dismissive behavior will interfere with the optimal healing process of the body.

Maybe I was wrong about the pills; maybe I was just being stubborn or proud; maybe I was acting habitually on the no-pill-taking values of my childhood. Finally, being cautious, I gave in. One week after I had talked with the surgeon, I called my primary-care physician and left a message with her advice nurse. The message asked my physician to recommend and refer me to anyone whom she wanted me to see. I told her that she knew me pretty well, so I would leave it up to her to pick the right person for me. The advice nurse called back the following day to tell me that my physician wanted to see me in her office.

On January 9th at 10:40 a.m. I arrived at the physician's office. I brought my manuscript with me. The first thing that the physician said when she entered the office was that the surgeon had called her after my appointment with him and that he was worried about me. That was a surprise to me.

"I know," I said, interrupting her comments, not wanting to hear more, "he thinks that I have secondary clinical depression."

"Do you think you do?" she asked.

"I don't think so, but if I am the only one who thinks I am okay, I had better pay attention to the rest of you."

She went down the list: Could I sleep? Could I eat? Could I make day-to-day decisions? Had I lost energy? Had I lost interest in the normal things that I did? I did not have a problem with any of them, except, maybe, the sadness that still appeared at times.

I showed her the manuscript and told her that it was what I had been working on for the past few months. I told her that I was still on my spiritual journey and that I was working very hard on that. I asked her if she wanted to read the manuscript. She accepted and at the same time said that she did not think that I was in depression and that she did not think that I needed to see anyone or get a prescription for chemical relief. We talked some more about the spiritual journey and once again she said that people usually did that sort of thing with a guide. I reminded her that she said that she would help when I needed it.

We agreed, on that visit, that I would return to the college on January 15th. She would have the medical release letter ready for me before then. If the sadness, indeed, was related to my refusal of the call to move forward on my journey of consciousness, I would just have to learn to live with it.

My family celebrated the end of my convalescence with a ski trip to Aspen. I had seen the pulmonologist the day before I saw my physician and the pulmonologist said that, while still on Coumadin to prevent further blood clots, I could do anything but cut myself or fall on my head. I asked specifically about skiing and he said only that I must be sure to ski under control.

I was a pretty good skier, but over the years I had become more cautious as well. I was extra-cautious on that trip because of the blood-thinning medication, so cautious in fact that Will, an expert skier, admonished me about the increased chance of accidents due to fear. Just before lunch on the first day, Ben spotted the photographer on the slopes and alerted him that our party would ski down one at a time to have our pictures taken individually. We already had made arrangements for our usual family photograph to be taken at the top of the mountain a little later.

Dave went first, but did not get the message about the photographer, so missed his photo-op. Each of the others took their turns before me. I was last. They all were waiting for me at the bottom of the slope, watching. I decided to make that my best run. I skied fast, with very nice form, and I looked pretty good. The photographer got a fine picture of me. And then it happened.

With Dave, back toward me, innocently gazing out over the valley, and the others facing me, I skied directly toward Dave, like a moth to the flame. I did not slow down, I did not try to turn, and I crashed right into him. I took him out. I hit him head to head! Both of us fell to the ground. The others could not believe what they had just seen. Not wanting to worry them, but being very aware of the pulmonologist's instructions, which must have been on my mind the entire time, I urgently whispered to Dave: "Get up, Dave, get up, quick; tell me if I am bleeding." And I was. My nose and eye had crashed directly into the back of Dave's head. My nose was cut and my eye already was beginning to darken. Dave was fine, startled, but fine.

By the time we stopped for lunch, I had a black eye. By the time we stopped skiing for the day, I had a fighter's "mouse." Ben made a point of noting that I had not even put my arms out in front of me to protect myself from the collision. By the end of the following day, there was so much blood in the sac that had formed under my eye that everyone insisted that I go to the emergency room to be examined and to have the blood siphoned out of the little sac. The emergency room doctor did all of the appropriate tests, used a needle to siphon the blood away from the eye, and released me into the care of my family.

A few days later I returned to the college, after being away for three months, with a real shiner. Most people were gracious enough not to ask. I told those who did ask that I had bumped into something.

It would have been more accurate, of course, to note that we bring into our lives whatever it is that we focus upon. I had been focusing on the fear of falling, and so I fell: another reminder not to focus on the negative in this experience, on the sadness or the loneliness, and, perhaps, on the fear of responding to the intuition.

In early March, Dave, Janet, one of my former students, and I took the Chinese exchange students and faculty skiing at Lake Tahoe. The students, from South China, had never before seen the snow coming down. It was a wonderful weekend and since the other three chaperones had heard the story of my black eye, all were careful not to turn their backs to me at the bottom of the runs.

Nor could I turn my back on the two surprising physical events that had lain in wait for me upon my return from my second stay in the hospital.

The Loneliness
(Existential Disconnection)

The two powerful physical events that I had undergone when I returned home from the hospital the second time were important facets of the entire experience. The first had involved physical spasms of sadness; the second had involved the physical feeling of being encased in loneliness. I was satisfied that the significance of the sadness was related to my intended refusal of the "call to adventure" and had accepted the fact that I would just have to learn to live with it. What was the loneliness all about?

I could not remember when I first had experienced loneliness. It certainly was not when I was a child. My life was so clearly supported by the love of my parents and my brother that loneliness never appeared in it. I did not remember ever feeling lonely as a child.

I decided that the first manifestation of anything like loneliness in my life occurred during my teenage years when I listened to classical music as I went to sleep at night. After a busy, fulfilling day, there was a yearning to be in contact with something higher, to place the experiences of the day within a greater context of meaning. In my high school years, I actively found the "something higher" in music, in literature, in the waves off the Southern California beaches, in intellectual pursuits, in achievement, in God. That yearning for higher contact could be called existential loneliness. It had appeared now and then in my adult life in periods when I did not seem to be fully committing my life energy to something bigger than myself.

It was not surprising that my college Master's thesis was written about Plato, the Greek philosopher who argues that there are multiple levels of reality and that the abstract, universal, intangible, unique, unchanging entities (forms) in the highest level are also the most real. The world that we live in, he had said, is made up of those abstract entities combined with illusion.

"Our world" includes physical, multiple, imperfect, impermanent, particular things; they are constantly changing and so this world is called the "world of Becoming." In our world, entities only appear to be what they are, and they do not last over time. The other world, the *real* world, is that highest level, the "world of Being," where entities really are what they seem to be and remain that way forever. What makes this hard for many people to accept is the recognition that Plato, like Berkeley, is saying that the most real world also is the intangible world, the non-physical world. Most people equate reality with physicality.

When I had listened to the music at the end of the day in those early years, I had been carried to the world of Platonic ideals, the world where "entities really are what they seem to be and remain that way forever." Art and drama and literature can take us there as well. So can mathematics. So can love. Just as it seemed that I was experiencing once again that existential loneliness, or yearning, for the "real world" in my current situation, my physician reminded me that spirituality must be carried out in this world, our world, and that I would have to deal with my immanent decision in both worlds.

A few nights later, I heard a speaker refer to that as "being tethered" to the world. She was referring to the needs of spiritual writers—a group I seemed to have entered—to remain grounded. No one *ever* had called me ungrounded. Nor was I at that point. So I was not worried about that. It seemed to me, that if my life were out of balance, it would be in the direction of paying too much attention to the physical world, not the spiritual world. I looked at the attachments that were preventing me from following the intuition that had called forth the sadness. Money, power, and status, are the stuff of this world. They are hardly spiritual ideas! I concluded that much of the loneliness of the surgical experience was existential loneliness. I clearly had some spiritual work to do in my future.

I also knew that there was another kind of loneliness that, perhaps, was more pressing at that time. It was the result of desiring to share important experiences with others. As members of a communal species, most of us like to share our important experiences with others. The companions whom I desired for those important experiences were not romantic partners or mates; rather they simply would be friends or acquaintances who were involved in the experience as deeply as I was, those who were walking the same path that I was walking at that time.

I really did not want to go through this alone.

Up until now I had had the good fortune of sharing my existential path with many such companions, all of them Platonic. The companion did not have to be permanent. Maybe I misread the energy, but I thought that the surgeon was one of those temporary partners. He called himself a partner. I did not expect him to be quite so temporary.

What was important for that partnership was that each of us had a lot invested in a common experience: my life and his talent. We were the only two people who had that combination for that experience. The experience was transcendent and powerful for me; looking back I could see later that it was not that significant for the surgeon. For me, the experience was not just a physical surgical experience; it was full of metaphysical import, of symbolic meanings. That was not true for the surgeon; for him, the experience was only about the surgery and its physical aftermath, *viz.* the excising of the problem and the healing of the wound, not even the healing of the person. He not only had a different perspective on that shared experience, but also he had not gone through the experience as intensely as I had. It was unique for me; it was one of many for him. What was life transforming for me was business as usual for the surgeon. It seems we had never been companions in a shared life experience.

I was all alone and a pervasive loneliness became an undercurrent of my life. Pema Chodron, the Buddhist nun whose books I had been reading, says that loneliness is the human condition. I did not like that. I loved independence and I loved being alone; I just did not like the feeling of existential loneliness, and I did not like the absence of a human spiritual companion at times when I was experiencing major life events. I did not like either kind of loneliness, but because of the work that I had been doing in trying to understand the events of the previous several months, I was getting closer to accepting them when they occurred. I still did not think of them as the way things must be. If I had designed the universe, I would not have designed it that way. The fact that I felt that surely meant that I did not yet understand the purpose of loneliness.

The weeks from early November until early December, marked my conscious and deliberate attempt to "lean into it," as both Pema Chodron and my physician would have said. It was my attempt to learn as much as I could about what was happening to me. That was not easy. *First, I could not go back, and now I had to work through this alone.*

The Abandonment
(Independence)

It had always been my opinion that the best energy relation is one in which each of the individuals is operating with full energy and is mutually sharing energy with another fully energized person. Ideally, that would be the optimal equal energy exchange. I encouraged that level of energy in my students, found it in my family, friends, and colleagues, and now I expected it in my surgeon.

My relationship with the surgeon was complicated by having characteristics of several different kinds of energy exchange. First, the surgeon was a being who had entered my life unsought by me. Within moments there was a bond, a relaxed comfortable energy bond that went in both directions, and that, combined with events of the surgical experience, reinforced a natural energy in me.

Next, as a result of the multiple physical shocks in the experience, the energy bond changed; the surgeon became some sort of lifeline for me. I began to need his energy and his protection. When the energy exchange became unequal, and when he did not notice that, my pleasure with his company turned into hurt and anger. The surgeon contributed to and intensified the change in energy level by his singular focus on the physical complications that followed the surgery and by his negative personal response to those complications: worry, annoyance, aggressive solutions, impersonal focus—"project mode" he would call it later. It was then that he withdrew the shared energy, then that he objectified my being, then that he withdrew my protection.

The loss of that coveted protection was a third important factor in my relationship with the surgeon. My desire for the surgeon's protection and my response when it was overtly denied eventually became one of the images that helped me transcend the surgical experience. I consciously chose to use the surgeon's withdrawal in that way. In the larger picture, however, for patients in general, the failure of a surgeon to protect both his patient's body and soul throughout the *entire* surgical experience is a callous and serious breech of the surgeon-patient relationship.

There was a fourth confounding factor in the situation, which made the analysis of my relationship with the surgeon that much harder. That final factor was my gratitude for the entry into my life of that person at that time: gratitude to him and gratitude to life in general. He was a very competent surgeon; he also was a very fine human being. I would learn an immense amount in the next few months because of him, and even though events had been different and much, much harder than I expected them to be, he eventually would come around and stand beside me for a while. I had trusted him from the beginning and by letting me down, he unknowingly had forced me to grow. Underlying my hurt and anger, and always there at some level, was my gratitude both to him and for him. That gratitude kept the hurt and anger in control. The warning from the gurney scene had worked.

Most of those four aspects in my relationship with the surgeon were disappointing for me: First, it had been suggested to me that there really was no initial energy sharing, that that had been a ploy on his part, his *modus operandi*; second, his withdrawal into project mode cut off the source of my needed energy; third, his being as a protector, while described by my physician as more caring than most, retrogressed toward what one of my very capable nursing friends called "cut-and-run" behavior; finally, only my gratitude remained untarnished and that was because I chose to seek metaphysical meaning in the experience rather than to quickly put it behind me and unthinkingly return to life as it had been before surgery. I committed myself to recognizing the important messages that I had received by way of the surgeon and the experience, and I tried to understand my responses to both. The metaphysical search for meaning saved me from the negative responses that came from the surgeon and softened the negative emotions his responses generated in me.

Even understanding that, however, at the moment, I desperately wanted someone to protect me on this journey and no one was there. On my own, all alone with respect to this experience, suffering miserably in both body and soul, I would later discover the connection between my desire for protection and my role as "damsel in distress." That knowledge came from Carolyn Myss' book, *Sacred Contracts*. Myss uses the Jungian language of archetypes. A major assignment in the first part of her book is for the reader to select eight archetypes that are most closely aligned with the reader's approach to life. That was an interesting and, at the time, comfortably distracting project. I dutifully followed the rules for completing the assignment. I even did a comparison between the set of archetypes that was related to my usual life and the set that was in place during the surgical experience. I knew that no archetype is intrinsically good or bad, that its value for our lives depends on our use of it.

I came across one archetype called the "vampire." The vampire archetype does just what one would think it would do: it feeds on the energy of people until they are left depleted:

"Oh, no! Drafting on energy . . . feeding on energy. Am I now a vampire?"

"Impossible," I laughed.

In fact, I did not seriously consider that to be one of my archetypes because it was very unusual for me to use others' energy and the description of the archetype simply did not fit my approach to life.

Another archetype, however—the "damsel in distress"—was definitely mine. Since I had grown up in an environment in which there was no need for self-protection, I had carried with me a high level of trust in other people, and also an assumption of their good will and its concomitant protection, hence the damsel in distress: If I ever needed help, someone would be there to provide it.

Look at the gurney scene: *there she is!* It could not be more obvious. I remembered describing the woman on the gurney as having no control over events that were about to take place and as *being quite comfortable with that*. Damn! My earlier analysis of the gurney scene had suggested that I had abdicated the emotional power of my being in favor of reason guided by my unconscious. Now, it appeared that, in real life, I had handed over that emotional energy to the surgeon!

I actually had given up my life energy to another person! I could not believe I had done that, especially to someone I knew nothing about. The spiritualist, whom I saw in November, had suggested that I felt hurt by the cancerous invasion and the blood clots to the lung because whoever took care of me in the spiritual universe had turned away for a moment, and I was unprotected for that period. Was I confusing the existential need to be safely connected to the universe with my human desire for a protector on the spiritual path? If the universe could not protect me, maybe the surgeon could?

It is one thing to be unprotected, another to abdicate one's personal power.

In the long run, the loss of the surgeon was good for me. The surgeon's withdrawal made me go through the entire transformation experience alone. Although I had immense support and love from my family and friends, it was *my* experience, just as my response now had to be *my* response, and that was the message that the surgeon had delivered to me.

I had wanted a partner for my surgical experience. Unfortunately, the only available partner for that experience was a surgeon who had not yet connected with the spiritual meaning of life. That probably answered the earlier question of why he was assigned to me, or I to him. His job, unbeknownst to him, was to force my independence; my job was to open his eyes to a more full world than the one in which he lived. If I listened and understood, I would elevate the level of my life. If he listened and understood, he would become a wise surgeon-healer, rather than just the expert surgeon that he was on his way to being.

Guidelines
(Joining The Symbols)

It was now January and my life, though reduced almost to nothing in outside responsibility, had been internally chaotic for several weeks. It had been a cacophony of thoughts, emotions, and, of course, the unwelcome intuition. I now needed to connect the emotions with the thoughts. I needed order. I needed creative, personal order.

I thought that my rational analysis of the images that had emerged during this period would provide that order and to a certain extent it did. The analysis, image by image, symbol by symbol, provided me a safe haven from my emotions and some insight into the import of the intuition. That had been my goal. There was no resolution, however, from the individual symbols about how to go beyond them, about what to do next.

Anyone who is involved in creative work of any kind knows that there are parts of it that cannot be pushed. The "Eureka" moment, the "Aha" moment, is as likely to come when one is driving the car, showering, or attending a football game, as it is to come during the deep concentration of the creative endeavor. At possibly one of the most important moments in my life, I could not hurry the "Aha" moment. I could only play with, sort, ruminate on, and intimately get to know both those thoughts and those emotions. I was a mystery to myself. I had the symbols, but no vision of their final relationship to each other—to me. I did not yet see the big picture.

What had begun as a simple intellectual distraction had become a need to find meaning in the surgical experience of the fall in order to get rid of emotions and find a response to the intuition. That search for meaning was turning into a challenging spiritual transformation of my life. The process involved my body, reason, emotion, intuition, a reassessment of my personal and professional life, and an examination of my world-view. It was time to bring the symbols together.

Beyond the actual physical experience, the first three symbols had been intellectual. The symbolism of the physical locations of my two health challenges had led me to consider where my *creativity* might be under attack and where my life *spirit* might be plugged. The symbolism of the gurney scene had suggested that the rational side of my personality, guided by my unconscious, was *protecting the emotional side of my personality*, and that the emotional side was about to be threatened by upcoming negative emotions.

The image of the surgeon was multi-faceted; sometimes intellectual, sometimes emotional, the image changed over time. *Intellectually*, I had learned from the entry of the surgeon into my life that something was lacking in my work in the world, something upon which I probably would not act. I also had learned intellectually that I was not living with the full *passionate intensity* that I knew I had in me and that I loved. *Emotionally*, I had come to need the energy of the surgeon to help me through the healing process and I had expected his protection. The intellectual facet of the surgeon symbolism was no more compelling than the other three intellectual symbols and could be put off until later. The emotional dependency on his energy was a big surprise to me, completely out of character for me, and of an intensity that both baffled and scared me. It made no sense to me. But, if that were all I had had to deal with, the story would have ended much sooner.

Immediately after my second surgery, the intuition arrived. I awoke from the surgery with the very strong intuitive sense that I could not return to my life as I knew it. There was a sense of danger in a refusal of that intuitive command, partly physical (the rash could recur, so could the blood clots) and partly spiritual (I could die with my music still in me). The life to which my intuition commanded me not to return could only be my professional life or my family life. I strongly believed that there was no way that I was going to leave either one of those parts of my life in search of *the promise that there is more in life*. That knowledge led to an immense emotional sadness about my likely refusal of the intuitive command, a refusal based upon *fear*.

At that time none of that was known to anyone but me. I tried to tell the surgeon, but that conversation did not work out. He had turned his focus to the infections that followed the interference of the chemically-thinned blood with the healing of the vulvectomy. Soon, the surgeon completely withdrew his interest in me as a person and turned me into a project, a thing. Even as I struggled to handle all of that by myself, I found myself abandoned and rejected at the very moment that I needed the most support. I discovered that the journey was one that I was going to have to *take by myself* and that led to an overwhelming sense of loneliness both spiritual and personal that signaled a *spiritual disconnection* in my life.

Those were the symbols that came from the eight images that I had chosen to analyze. There they were all together. Together they led to guidelines for my next step in conscious growth. They influenced a decision that needed to be made, a decision about the intuition that would certainly affect my work and my family, but that also would transform my being. That was not all bad. If anything, the chaotic mix of thoughts, emotions, and intuitions had an aura of adventure, challenge, and excitement to it. I had been eager to meet the players in the chaos and to get to know them, because deep down inside I knew that I was the creative project. I had just been given the opportunity to recreate my entire life.

For years, in jest, I had asked for a duck. The duck that I wanted was like the one on the Groucho Marx show in the 50s. Groucho agreed with the audience about a word that would be kept secret from the contestant. When, in conversation with Groucho, the contestant unsuspectingly uttered the secret word, a toy duck would drop on a cord from the ceiling holding in its mouth a card with the word inscribed on it. The contestant then won a prize for having stumbled upon the word in conversation.

I had wanted a life-duck, one that would fall from the sky and direct me to my destiny when I unexpectedly came upon a fork in the road. Knowing the rules of the game I would be nudged from the wrong direction by the absence of the duck, or reaffirmed in my choice of direction by the life-duck that would fall from the sky right at my feet. And now, it seemed, my analysis had lured a duck to my path—finally—one holding not a single word, but a set of guidelines for me, guidelines that came from bringing together the eight images and their symbolic meanings for me.

The most recent phase of your life is over. It is time to move forward on your personal journey. You are to find a new way to contribute to the world, a way that draws forth your creativity and your spirit even further than before, a way that immerses your life in passionate existence. Though it may be hard to leave your beloved former life, though the decision may be hard to make, it is essential that you include your emotions in the decision, but only those emotions that are positive. If you do not heed this message, you will succumb to the sadness of an unfilled life, for you will know that you have chosen to miss your destiny. Loneliness will follow as you try to fill the void in your existence with moments in the transcendental world. No one will tell you what to do; you must create the next phase of your life by yourself. You are totally responsible for the life that you are about to choose!

I sat down on my path, stunned. It was not the guidelines that caught my attention so dramatically. They were no surprise; after all, I had been working with them symbol by symbol for weeks. I was stunned, instead, by my resistance, by my inability simply to follow them. Would I rather stay in the grips of those negative emotions of sadness and loneliness than seek passionate existence? What did I have to lose?

Well, my job and career for starters, money, prestige, achievement, and the opportunity to make a contribution. That is not an insignificant list! But what did I have to gain? Nothing less than a passionate life, even more creative work, joy, independence, personal power. How sure was I about those losses and gains? Really sure about the losses, not so sure about the gains.

And that was the rub; even though I now had guidelines to help determine where I was going, I was not sure that I had the courage to follow them.

OPERATING

External Pressure

Something had to be missing, some image ignored, some symbol overlooked. I could not get the surgeon's insult out of my mind. I could not assuage the loneliness. I could not find the courage to move on from my current professional position. I had tried rational thought and though my beloved reason had sorted out the problem and given me a solution and a set of guidelines, it had not given me enough motivation to act. The level of the challenge had just escalated. Reason would no longer be enough.

The missing motivation for responding to the intuition was trust, but I did not know that at the time. It was one of three positive emotions that lay quietly in my being, that had been infused in me in my earliest days of life, decades ago. Those positive emotions had been shaken but reaffirmed by the events of the fall, and they soon would overpower the negative emotions about which I had been warned. Trust was the first of those positive emotions; commitment and love were the others. Trust and commitment were to resurface first. They would bring with them the decision about following the intuition, the decision about leaving the college, and the acceptance of all the symbols hidden in the images.

Reason had given me everything that I needed to understand the choice to follow the intuition and more specifically to address the decision about leaving the college, everything, that is, except a guarantee against any personal risk or the necessary commitment to actually make the decision.

I was caught between the emotions of sadness and loneliness that refused to go away and the new emotion of fear that was beginning to appear. Now, in mid-January, my rational analysis seemed to be at a standstill, but that was not really so. Negative emotions had never been a big part of my life; I also was listening closely to the warning to excise them from my life altogether, so my situation, though painful, was not as bad as it might have seemed. I might have been moving at the speed of a snail, but I was moving.

I felt that I was making progress in figuring out how to handle the events of the fall when, six weeks after the surgery, the outside pressures began. They were subtle at first: people asking if I had gone back to work yet and expressing surprise when I said no; the college president saying that he did not want me to work anymore at home; the HR director of the college asking repeatedly for a medical leave of absence application; the same HR director sending a formal letter stating that the work that I had done at home (over a month's work in hourly calculations) would not be credited to me and then calling again to say that because of a mistake in the business office calculations, I now owed the college money for my time off (after 23 years of service with rare absences)! My accrued vacation time was also being challenged.

Everybody wanted an answer; it seemed as if everybody wanted me to be who I had been, or at least to be predictable, to be settled. I needed to be fluid. I was in the midst of the dance of response. "To be or not to be," was not the only game in town. As even the early Greek philosophers knew two thousand years ago, becoming matters: I was being challenged "to become or not to become."

Even as I was still trying to find a rational response to the challenge to become or not to become, I knew at some level that becoming is a spiritual question. I should not confuse it with an emotional or rational question. Becoming is a challenge for the soul, one that can only be answered by total life commitment. I knew enough to realize that a conditional answer would not work, that a "yes" answer required a leap of faith and absolute trust—no fear. I also realized that fear was sneaking in.

By now I knew that this was not just a creative process. It also was a process of commitment. I understood that. I needed time.

Your Time Is Up

"You have five more minutes before your time is up. This would be a good time for you to jot down the points which you have yet to discuss, summarize, and then draw your conclusion."

How many times had I said that as I proctored a college examination? Groans, frustration, panic from some of the students, silent focus from others as they intently pulled together their thoughts and marshaled their arguments. Then,

"Your time is up! Please pass your blue books up to the front of the room."

The younger students in their first year often wrote "TIME" in huge letters at the end of the essay that they had not finished. That not-so-subtle message to me, the professor, translated into:

"I know more than I can tell you I know. Please have sympathy for me."

And I did have sympathy, probably not the way they hoped, however. I graded the essays according to the merits of the essay, both content and form, but then subsequently I spent considerable time beyond the content of the course teaching them how to express themselves and their arguments in a concise, logical way so that time would no longer be an issue for them.

I probably learned how to do that during all my years as a student. I loved being a student. My last student adventure had been a return to Stanford in the early 90s to earn a post-doctoral Master's Degree in International Policy Studies. I did that while teaching full time and chairing the Psychology Department at my college. I took a course or two each term at Stanford, which was allowed for full-time educators in the Bay Area. Sometimes that was a stretch, like the six terms that I enrolled for the 8:00 a.m. Japanese language course at Stanford and managed to be down the street in my own college classroom by 9:10 a.m. to teach my classes there.

My favorite course in that period at Stanford, bar none, was one taught by Professor Stephen Krasner of the Political Science Department. It was such a popular course that the students flocked to it. Six or seven hundred students filled Dinklespiel auditorium and its balconies. Professor Krasner carried a microphone with a cord. He was an artist. He was like a stand-up comedian. The cord became a prop as he stepped over it, twirled it, or trailed it behind as he paced across the stage. Professor Krasner was brilliant, intense, articulate, funny, and captivating. I could not wait to get to his class every afternoon, 699 eighteen-to-twenty-two-year olds and me.

The course was called "How Nations Deal With Each Other" and it included the paradigms or models of international relations and their philosophic bases. Toward the end of the course we took a few issues, like the causes of World War I, for example, and assessed them from each of the paradigms. So, for example, was World War I caused by states and the distribution of power, by classes and class interest, by institutions embodying values and beliefs, by bureaucracies or individuals satisfying psychological needs, or by some combination of those? Professor Krasner taught us that there are multiple ways of looking at the same international issue and that each of those ways rests upon a set of assumptions, which if rationally organized we call a paradigm or model.

I thought of the elephant story in which seven blind wise men come across an elephant, a kind of being of which they have never heard. They surround the elephant and attempt to determine what it is by touching it. The one holding the elephant's tail declares this thing to be a rope. The one touching the ear decrees it to be a fan. The one with his arms around the leg claims that the thing is a tree. The one at the elephant's side decides that they have come upon a wall. And so on for the other three.

Were they wrong? Yes and no. What each had was a part of the truth. What none of them had was the whole truth. The error was not in the perception, or even in the description, but in the belief that any one of them had the entire being in his grasp. So it was with the blind men and the elephant. So it is with most people's approach to international relations. So it could be with my attempt to explain what had happened to me in the fall of 2001. I had one interpretation of the event. Someone else might have a different interpretation. In the end, I hoped to find some truth in my story based on my assumptions. Others would find their truth based on their assumptions. If we kept sharing these kinds of experiences, we could all get closer to the ultimate truth.

By early December when the pressure from the external world became too much I wanted to shout "TIME," just as my students had done. I needed more time. I was not yet ready to make life-changing decisions. The stakes of the life exam I was taking were too high. But worse, I recognized that I had studied for the wrong course. I was prepared for a simple psychological analysis of my response to events. I thought that, along the way, I would be reminded of some earlier knowledge, apply it, and overcome the trauma. But it was not a psychological experience any more than it was a physical experience. I was involved in a spiritual experience.

I had walked into a crash course in Spiritual Transformation and I did not have the prerequisites. It was not a rational course; it required intuitive skills, not rational skills. Out the window, by demand, went logic, prudence, and rational calculation, skills that I had mastered well. I had the horrible realization that I was not prepared, that I might flunk the test, or worse, that I simply might not show up for the exam. If anybody needed to write "TIME" in her exam booklet, it was I. It was not that I would not find an answer eventually; it was that I did not have an answer then and life was calling "TIME!"

Six weeks was the usual time for recovery for those kinds of surgeries. If one counted my second surgical procedure as the beginning of the six weeks, I would have been expected to return to work in mid-December. That, indeed, was the time of the President's comment and the beginning of the pressure from the HR Department at the college. My son, Will, was also wondering why I had not returned to work yet. Even my husband, Dave, questioned my decision to delay my return until after the New Year.

It was easy to answer the surface questions about time: I had decided to return to the college after the New Year because the end of the fall semester was December 14th and the administrative offices were closed during the Christmas break. Furthermore, I did not have a medical release yet from my physician or my surgeon. Physically, I was still in great discomfort; I would not find out about the status of the blood clots in the lung until after Christmas; and the 27th of December marked the date that I was supposed to return to the surgeon for the three-month check-up.

The reason for the close monitoring of the wound site was the high rate of early recurrence of the Paget's Extra-mammary Disease, about 45%. I had told the surgeon much earlier, in what started as a light conversation, that I did not expect the disease to recur but that if it did, I would opt for another physical location (obviously). His response was that its return and the location were not up to me. He then launched into a description of one situation that his partner, a famous surgeon, currently was handling, in which the genital rash had not only returned, but had returned directly to the graft site in the wound. With that image in mind, I called my physician's office to ask about the medical release that I had to have in order to return to the college. When she called me back, I told her that I simply was not ready to return.

All I wanted to do from early December until mid-January and beyond was to write "TIME" in the universe's exam book, to show that I knew more about what was going on in my life than I could demonstrate at the moment.

Hurry Up

Why was it taking so long? I was haunted by the speed with which a self-actualized individual bounces back from a lower level difficulty according to Abraham Maslow's theory. According to Maslow, one measure of the level of self-actualization of an individual is the speed with which he or she recovers from a lower-level difficulty. Abraham Maslow was one of my favorite psychologists because he studied people who lived life at the highest human level rather than studying those who are having trouble even reaching the common or usual level of life experience.

Maslow says that all human beings have six levels of human need: physiology, safety and security, belonging, self-esteem, rational stimulation, and esthetic surroundings. He claims that a person must be fulfilled at each level before going on to the next level. Maslow is not interested in the rate of progress, only in the order of the progress. We share the first four levels, the basic needs, with other animals. The two highest levels, the esthetic and the cognitive, are what distinguish us as humans from the other animals.

Self-actualized individuals are those who spend a lot of their time in the two upper levels of the hierarchy. When they experience a disruption at the level of a basic need, they descend to that level, solve the problem, and return to the level of human needs, *viz.* the needs for rational stimulation and esthetic surroundings.

Dan Millman's book, *The Way of the Peaceful Warrior*, includes the example of a person who owns a restaurant. The restaurant unexpectedly burns to the ground while the owner watches. The hero of the story, Dan himself, observes how the owner deals with this loss. Dan is startled when the owner falls to the ground on his knees and lets out a wail, almost animalistic in nature, which lasts about a minute. Then the owner stands up and when asked what he is going to do, he calmly says that he has been thinking of going to Southern California sometime and that this seems like a good time to do that: No feeling sorry for himself. No wondering what to do next. No falling into sadness or lamenting the loss. Just moving forward in acceptance and trust.

The restaurant owner had fallen from wherever he was on Maslow's hierarchy of needs to the level of safety and security, the level at which restaurants burn down, cars are stolen, and thieves prowl the neighborhood. His intense keening was all the mourning that he needed. It was not that he did not care very much; it was that that intense minute was all that he needed. It was a matter of intensity of response, not duration of response.

I really thought that I was going to go through the surgery in that way. I had lived most of my life in the intellectual realm. Surely I could drop down for a week or two to solve a basic physical need at the lowest level of needs and then move right back up to where I had been before. Not so. As I began the ascent from the most basic level of need, the physiological, I was pushed back down again by the blood clots and the infections. Even then, my descent into the basic needs of physiology actually did not last long, especially with the positive news that the genital rash was non-cancerous and that the blood clots were under control for the time being. It was not long before I was working again on the hospital bed and then at home, back to intellectual pursuits. Surprisingly, far harder for me than the physical concerns were the issues of safety and security, belonging, and self-esteem.

On my way up again, the intuition slowed me down at the level of the needs of safety and security (Was I ready to give up money and independence?) and belonging (Would I really give up my academic community?). Finally, the surgeon imprisoned me for a time at the level of the need for self-esteem (How *could* he treat me as only an object?). Multiple hits, not just one. It took three months in total, not one minute as with the restaurateur, and I did my share of keening as well. I clearly did not have my act together as much as I thought that I did. That was a message in itself and I had not even counted that one as one of the images! To be fair to myself, any one of those images, in itself, would have signaled a single test of self-actualization.

Along the way to self-actualization individuals can open themselves to peak experiences. Maslow describes a peak experience as an experience of transcendence. It momentarily transports the individual out of life as he or she knows it. In the moment of the experience, the individual experiences the oneness of all existence. These moments can be found in musical, artistic, religious, interpersonal, athletic, or sexual experiences, to name just a few. A person knows whether the experience has been a peak experience by the way he or she views the world after the experience. The peak experience permanently changes the person's life.

My life certainly had been changed. Had my surgical experience been a peak experience? I was different from the person I had been in September; that was true. I had had many moments in which I had felt a deep connection with the world, but none of them had been transcendent in the sense that I either was totally immersed in the world, or completely moved beyond the world, beyond consciousness of where I was—that is, if I did not count the anesthesia.

But something interesting along that line occurred in the weeks following the surgery: I found myself wanting to be in the presence of the ideal: the best music, most beautiful art, deepest discussions, most esthetic surroundings, highest literature, most peaceful moments, most passionate energy. It was as if I had been in touch with some universal essence, some new level of reality, or some passion that I had been seeking for a long time.

I went through a couple of months during which I probably was an enigma to those who knew me well: I deliberately stayed away from situations or places of low energy, places of negative passivity; I missed meetings, events, and celebrations, and found a way to remove myself from those closest to me unless they had such energy. Many members of my family are filled with passionate energy, so are several of my former students and friends, not to mention Ben's dog, Professor Higgins, so I had a community.

If my experience had been a peak experience, it could have happened at any level of human need, and the changes in my being would endure. Thinking of Maslow was a positive thing for me. He also led me to realize that even if I did not have the ground under my feet as firmly as I thought that I had, I needed to get moving anyway.

My journey had begun and the call had been forceful. The meaning of my story was now almost completely clear, the guidelines were in place, yet so far I had declined to accept their message for my life. The internal emotional and intuitional pressures of warning, sadness, and loneliness still pushed hard for a resolution that I had not yet made. Eventually, and as part of the escalation, the external pressures had begun. Yet, still I stalled. Talk about resistance to change. Talk about fear.

It was time to get on with it, approach the decision head on. If I did not address that challenge, if I did not make my own decision about my future life, the decision would be made for me; time would make sure that happened. Time is the king of external pressures.

What was that delightful metaphor of Kierkegaard's? The horses are running on madly with no driver to direct them, while the driver sleeps in the wagon behind. It is time to wake up, Diane. Get on the driver's seat. Take control of the horses. No more sleeping in the wagon.

The Transition

Someone else was grabbing the reins!

I was caught off guard. The external pressures of time that began in early December were a surprise to me. It seemed obvious to me, that if someone were considering a major life change for the better, then, whatever the design of the universe, that life change would be supported. Since then I have read in several books that exactly the opposite happens. When one makes a major spiritual life decision, events immediately appear that test the sincerity and resolve of the decision.

I did not know that I had made any decision, let alone a spiritual decision. I certainly had made no conscious decision by early December—no conscious decision perhaps, but I had received the intuition openly and by doing so had set in motion a powerful response based upon earlier spiritual commitments in my life. There was never any question about my trust in the validity of the intuition; the question was about the strength of my will to follow its command. That too involved trust. You can't rush trust.

The call had come. I had been enthusiastically waiting for the "call to adventure" and when it came I panicked; I ran from it in fear. I hid from it in reason instead of responding from my heart; I was Jonah at the bottom of the boat. I did not like the external pressure, though it probably was a good turn of events for me. Having finally drawn all of the symbols together, I wanted to savor the decision. I wanted it to be *my* decision. I wanted my decision to be a conscious, rational decision, a decision under my control. I lived in my head a lot during that period. I was the perfect example of the introspective, introverted thinker when I was not personally engaged with other people. I was the model of a college professor.

Especially then, as a professor, reason told me that we must distinguish between intuitions and the actions that are based upon them. Historically, some horrendous actions had been justified by appeals to intuition. Even as I trusted the validity of my intuition, I knew that others had trusted their intuitions and that a single individual's intuition could change the course of human events or wreak havoc on the world. I sought to optimize human life, and I had a strong respect for individual freedom, so I was not worried about my intuition leading to egregious acts, but as a philosopher I knew that there is a great body of literature and thought devoted to the role of intuition as the basis of knowledge.

When one asks, "What is the role of intuition as the basis of knowledge?" he or she is exploring the appropriateness of the fourth circle. This stands as one of the most important questions in the world today, since it questions the sovereignty of rational constraints that guide the arguments among religions, and since it challenges the assumptions of the third circle as well.

There is another related and more specific question: "What is the role of intuition as the basis of philosophical knowledge?" This question lies at the very root of ethics: the study of good and evil, and right and wrong. In particular, it asks whether goodness or rightness is the most basic concept in ethics: is an act good because it is right or is it right because it brings about the greatest amount of good? And equally as important: if an act is right in itself—regardless of whether it brings about the greatest amount of good—how do we know its rightness? Do we *intuitively* know that it is right?

I clearly had moved through the circles of knowledge at this point: I was paying attention to and following the guidelines of the empirical Western medical world and a staunchly empirical surgeon (circle one); I had used reason to help me understand the significance of the events to my life (circle two); I had emotionally and spiritually acknowledged the intuition (circle four) and was succumbing for a while to the two negative emotions that followed. I recognized, finally, that I had gone beyond both emotion and reason in this experience and was standing on the cusp of two possible lives tangent to my spiritual journey (circle three).

Here on the cusp I knew that I had trusted the universe and yet I had contracted Paget's Extramammary Disease. Here on the cusp I knew that I had trusted the surgeon and that he had turned away from me when I needed him. Here on the cusp I asked why I should trust again. And here on the cusp I knew what the answer was; it was not hard to find: The answer was that I not only should, but would, trust again because I was in love. I was in love with life. And with love comes trust.

Trust

Clarity and certainty arrived along with the love, trust, and commitment. I would discover later exactly what I was supposed to do in the future. Right now I merely needed to make sure that the horses were taking me in the right direction.

Rationally, I had begun that process by thinking that attention to the symbolism in my experience might teach me something to improve my life. I never once thought that I would learn that I should give up the life that I was living. Even when I realized that was happening, there were moments when I thought that I would not have to give up my work, but that I myself would have to change: I would have to give up my expectancies, desires, and attachments. In truth, I was going to have to give up some, if not all, of those *as well as* my work.

Underneath everything—all the emotions and thoughts—was me, the essence of me, and I was okay; I had always been okay and would continue to be okay, no matter what. I was not in the slightest bit worried about that. But, directly outside of me, beyond me, was the unrelenting loneliness, not underneath as I understood it to be from Pema Chodron, but immediately surrounding the essence of me. Around the loneliness was the intuition. Around the intuition was the sadness that had lessened, but that still appeared from time to time, especially if I was not focused on finding the meaning of the experience and an answer to my dilemma. Around the sadness were the rest of the symbols. Beyond that, on the surface, was life as usual.

Of course, it was not life as usual; it looked like life as usual, and I often carried it off as life as usual, but it really was life as unusual, with one exception: when I was personally interacting with other people, I focused intently on what they were telling me. Rarely did I carry on an inner dialogue while listening to other people. I always thought that I was a good teacher; maybe, like Vasudeva, Siddhartha's mentor on the river, I was a good listener as well.

At that time, the best metaphor for my being was a globe or a hologram, with me, the essence of me, in the center. Whatever I was in the center, whatever was my essence, I had continually been assured that I was okay.

What about essences? Our second Great Pyrenees, Dizzy, the great-grandfather of Professor Higgins, taught us about essences. Great Pyrenees are immense dogs covered with beautiful white fur. They look like small Polar Bears with drooping ears. Dizzy's essence, we decided, was in the white spot at the lower tip of his left ear. The rest of his ear was a very light tan color. We loved Dizzy immensely. If there was any question about which of us Dizzy loved the most, we dove for the ear. Whoever could hold the white spot on the ear could claim to be with "the essence of the bear." The essence of "the bear" was love. Anyone who knows dogs knows how much the essence of a dog is love. When Dizzy passed away and it was my turn to say thank you and good-bye, I remembered my last touch as holding the white spot on the ear, at one with the essence of the bear.

Now, I was preparing to say thank you and good-bye to something else in my life. I did not think that it was going to be a good-bye to me, to who I really was, to my essence. Rather, I was preparing to say good-bye to what I had passed through, to some part of life that had been valuable to me, but was no longer where I was supposed to be. Even as I thought about saying good-bye, I realized that, indeed, some decision had been made on another level. I had listened to the call and was preparing to follow it. It was time to give up my old life. There was nothing rational about that: it was a leap of faith, a release of fear, a complete surrender, in that order.

That surrender would require the release of all of my recently discovered attachments: money, status, power, passionate intensity, and love. That was one of the lessons of the intuition. Following the intuition would require my jumping directly into the cauldron of my personal fears. Unless I released the fear that was attached to the loss or further growth of any of those attachments I would bungle the whole response.

Releasing the fear depended upon my trust that everything would work out when I did so, relinquishing my hope that it would work out the way that I wanted. Release of fear at that level is complete release of outcomes. Kierkegaard did a brilliant analysis of that act when he considered the case of Abraham preparing to sacrifice Isaac. Isaac was born to Abraham and Sarah quite late in their lives. Isaac was a great blessing to Abraham, who was a man of God. When Isaac was about ten years old, God commanded Abraham to sacrifice Isaac instead of the usual sacrifice of a lamb. One can imagine the agony that Abraham must have gone through. Leaving one's work in the world would be nothing compared to what Abraham had been asked to do.

Abraham took Isaac to the mountain and prepared the sacrificial altar. Isaac noticed that there was no lamb and asked his father about that. Abraham told Isaac that God had asked him to prepare Isaac to be the sacrifice. Great works of art portray Isaac's response differently; some show Isaac passively lying on the altar; others show him struggling, but either way, Kierkegaard's analysis is not about Isaac, but about Abraham. Abraham raises his arm to plunge the knife into Isaac and begins the downward stroke. As Abraham's arm comes down in what will be the fatal blow, the hand of God appears and stays Abraham's arm. At that very moment, a lamb appears from out of the sparse bushes on the mountain.

Kierkegaard's question was whether Abraham *had to believe with certainty* that he was going to sacrifice Isaac in order for God to intervene.

SOUL SURGERY

Would God have intervened if Abraham had expected Him to? Did God's intervention depend on Abraham's commitment to sacrificing Isaac unconditionally? Did my surrender to the intuition mean giving up those things to which I was attached, believing that I would never get them back? Thinking that the release of my attachments ultimately would bring them back to me would have been like crossing my fingers behind my back when I made a promise. A complete surrender would require 100% trust that everything would be okay, not that what I surrendered would be returned to me, but that everything would be okay. Fear is an indication of the lack of trust in the "okay-ness" of our future.

The validity of the intuition was not a concern for me; more worrisome were the consequences of acting on the intuition. That was the fear issue. Beyond that, however, was the awareness that once having surrendered, having acted, I would be required to check each and every one of my motives, to examine my very being, before setting out again to discover what I was to do in the next quadrant of my life.

I had no trouble with the idea of going through that internal examination. I well knew that there would be no point in giving up my position just to get a different position, no point in doing it all over again. Examples abound of people who leave jobs—or relationships—only to replace them with other jobs containing the same issues. I was certain that the decision on my part was not to be about an exchange, but about a different level of life somehow. Just as most people at my stage of life would be anticipating retirement after a successful career and family life in order to rest and enjoy the remainder of their lives, I would be going on another assignment. There was more that I had to do, but first I still had to find out who I really was.

I was the elephant! The Diane of that transitional time would be one whom many others had not met before. Each of those others would have his or her own perception of who Diane might be at that time, of what might have been prompting her decision making:

"Secondary clinical depression," would say one.

"Job burnout," another.

"She's had a spiritual call," a third would offer.

"No, no," the next would insist, *"It's the effect of the residual anesthetic in her body."*

"Diane's retiring!" would announce one.

"This is what happens when you don't protect your emotions," the next.

"She's worried about her life and the recurrence of the two illnesses," might suggest the seventh.

"Must have been the surgeries," would pronounce another.

"It was the way the surgeon treated her," would declare the last.

In contrast to the characters in the elephant story, the wise people in my life had the wisdom to ask me what was going on: Ask the elephant what it is. The physician and the rest of my guides all asked, as did all of my friends. The surgeon had made up his own mind.

My answer was that as wonderful as my life had been to that point and was at the moment, there was something more that I was supposed to be doing. I did not know what that was. It might not be showy or seem big, it might not be lucrative; it probably would use my talents, but might not; it might not seem to be a contribution, but it would be. I would not discover what it was that I was supposed to be doing until I had made myself ready to do it. The preparation would not be a passive period of doing nothing, but an intense period of examining those attachments, checking my motives for anything that I did, and trying to find out who I was, trying to get in touch with my essence. I wished that I had a white spot on *my* ear.

The lessons of the intuition were love, trust and commitment, dispensing with fear, and giving up attachments. Following the intuition would also be about patience. The surgeon had said that I would have to be patient with the healing of the wound. The physician had said that I would need to learn how to listen and to be patient. Siddhartha said that he could think, he could fast, and he could wait. I could think and I could fast. I was learning how to wait.

The Decision

From early December through mid-January, the topic of family conversation moved dramatically from the images to my response to symbolism. I, the person who was being forced to go through the experience alone, had the most generous, loving, and caring guidance from my immediate family, my extended family, a few close friends, and my physician. They would call when I least expected and most needed the call. They were inexhaustible. They were passionately involved, and they offered responsible and inspired counsel. Almost all of them felt that it was time for me to move beyond my work at the college.

I had long and many conversations with Ben and Will and Dave. My conversations with the three of them straddled the transition between the healing of the physical wound with its emotional and spiritual counterparts and the decision-making about my future, about the future of me. Dave was the most cautious of the three of them because it was also about the future of his wife. Will and Ben were marvelously objective and only considered the future of me as a person they loved, not the future of their mom. That was fitting; sons need to become independent from their moms, anyway, in ways not expected of husbands.

Dave was the first person I had told about the intuition. His immediate response was that it was silly, that there was no way that I was going to die, that it made no sense to say that my going back to life as usual was any threat to me. Those "endangered" emotions of mine surfaced to support me as I tried to explain. The explanation that Dave, an empiricist, was most likely to accept was the physical explanation that the stresses of the environments in question could lead to recurrence either of the Paget's Extra-mammary Disease or the pulmonary emboli, a thought that was part of my understanding of the intuition, but not the powerful message of the intuition. He understood the physical interpretation. He did not think that it was likely, but he understood it. What he did not understand was the other interpretation of the intuition: that I had a personal growth path and that somehow, sometime, some place, I had stopped traveling and was now resting by the side of the path, that it was time now for me to get up and start walking again.

That would be a hard concept for a spouse to accept unless the spouse also thought in terms of personal life journeys. It would be hard because, without such an understanding, there could be the anxiety, in traveler's language, of being left behind. I believed that everyone is on a journey, whether he or she consciously knows it or not. Not everyone chooses to move forward on his or her journey throughout his or her life, but that choice, too, is part of the journey. I certainly had not consciously and continuously focused on my journey every moment throughout my life. I had stopped and rested by the side of the road for certain periods of time, though the journey was always in my consciousness. People who do not see their lives as journeys often focus more on doing rather than being; even those consciously on journeys can do that. I had done that. I was only back on the path because a variety of helping circumstances scrambled out of the bushes and pushed, pulled, and dragged me onto the path once again.

I knew that no one can make the choice to take the journey for anyone else. Jung says that one of the advantages of a long-term, monogamous relationship is that each individual is able to be him- or herself without the threat of the other one walking away. That was where Dave and I were right then. I expressed the need to go on my journey of consciousness; Dave had no interest in such a journey at that time.

Both of us respected the other's choices, although neither of us was happy with those choices; we respected them, but wished they had been different.

Respecting the choices, I was careful to maintain enthusiasm for daily topics that were no longer of interest to me, to try not to be insensitive to the importance of what Dave wanted to talk about or do. He, in turn, helped me figure out the practical ramifications of my choice: budgets, financial plans, how life would change because of the loss of my income. As different as we were and as different as our life paths were, there was an unspoken level of trust and friendship that lay underneath, a recognition of a commitment not to harm and a commitment to assist when we could.

My sons were wonderful during that period. They were my strongest supporters. The most powerful support that they gave me was simply their confidence that I would be fine no matter what I did, that I had great gifts to offer the world, and that those gifts would be accepted: my talents would be actualized. But they gave me more than that. During that time, they spent time on the phone with me responding to every little argument that I had, addressing with me every little fear that I had. They pointed out the obvious and the not so obvious. They were ruthlessly objective and compassionately involved at the same time. They were my counselors; they were my guides for this stage; they were my sons. Almost every conversation during that period led to the question of what Mom had decided to do. Their position was: Do it; make a choice and carry it out. When pushed for what they thought that I should do, they told me that I already had made up my own mind and that it was time now to accept that, to *act* on my decision.

I would have liked to stall forever.

Time would not let me do that. I ached inside with the immensity of the decision about resigning from the college. So much of my life was there; so much of me was there. I loved being a teacher; I passionately created the international center; I cherished my students, my alumni friends, my colleagues there and in China, my books, abstract ideas. I valued the guys from maintenance and information technology. I was committed to my staff. I loved all of that, but I needed to move on.

My physician had been the single most powerful influence in my returning to the college. She, of course, was not the keeper of the clock, but she did have to sign the release for my return to the college.

"Diane," she had said, "the answer about whether or not you still belong there will come to you more easily when you are there. You will find your answer faster from the college than from the glass-topped table on your deck."

"I am afraid that I will get lured into the mechanics of the everyday again, that I will forget this experience, that I will settle, that it will be life as usual, that I will turn my back on my journey," I lamented.

"That won't happen," she responded. "This has been too powerful for that. You are different now. Maybe that difference will help change the college; maybe they will change too. Maybe you no longer belong at the college. You can only find that out at the college."

As the date to return to the college came closer, I became more and more reluctant to return. There was not a specific moment of conscious choice to leave the college; but it became increasingly more apparent to me that I was going to accept the call, go on the journey, and leave the college. By Monday morning, January 15, I knew that I was going to resign. The dread turned into peace. I had made up my mind. The irrevocable decision had been made in my heart. It was not calculated; it was not prudent; it was not rational. Now, what remained was only the question of how to resign well: how to honor the college and the people in it, how to leave the international center in such good shape that it could sustain the shock of my leaving, how to say good-bye with grace.

Once again, I turned to my sons for guidance. Humorous as they were, accomplished, young, prudential, energetic, and intelligent, they also knew about grace. They became the protocol advisors on any and all issues that came up during that time, especially on the negative ones that came out of some of the college offices. No issue that arose became confused with the purpose of my leaving and my commitment to doing it with grace. I was making that move with 100% focus.

The clarity of the decision had an inverse relationship to the strength of the sadness that I had experienced. The closer I had come to making the decision, the less frequent and less powerful were the visits of sadness, until one day the decision had been made and the sadness was gone. In the months that followed the decision, I would find that I did not once regret the decision that I had made. Sometimes a general emotion might appear out of nowhere, unrelated to the decision, and if I had not been careful I might have thought that it was the sadness; but I knew better from paying close attention to those feelings: it was the loneliness. The sadness had not been about the college; it had been about the possibility of my rejecting the call. Resolution of the loneliness would not appear for a few more months.

I had begun the adventure as an intellectual and psychological assessment of a physical experience. Somehow I had stumbled onto a spiritual journey and had tried to go through that alone, without a personal guide. Probably recognizing how much assistance and support I would need, whoever arranges life in the universe sent me a coterie of guides to help me through the experience and to set me back on the road again. Some of the guides were people; others were experiences. The images were guides. Even the family's bird, cat, and Professor Higgins were guides. Everything spoke to me; there was meaning everywhere.

By the time I made the decision, I knew that the intuition was a call of some sort, but one with no specific instructions. I also knew that refusing or ignoring a "call to adventure" would exact a big price. In response to the intuition, I knew that I needed to find new creative work in the world and I knew that the work needed to support the spiritual evolution of the world. I knew that the energy for that work would not come solely from me, but through me, and that it would be inexhaustible.

The decision-making period was over. That probably had been the hardest part of the adventure. Erik Erikson, the psychologist, talks about the human drive for growth, the "epigenetic principle," and how it manifests itself in these kinds of choices. He speaks of how we have a sense of the impending change and how we want both the change and the security of the *status quo* at the same time. He points to the transitions of the two-year old and the young adolescent as clearly visible struggles with the impossibility of having our cake and eating it too. Just as the two-year old and the adolescent react tumultuously to their impossible desires, to the process, so I often had kicked and screamed internally as I went through the process as well.

I was well aware that we have to give up where we are to get to where we are going. I had spent three months in the land of transition, wanting what I could not have, wanting both growth and security at the same time. I knew at that point that there was no turning back. Whatever the future held, there was no possibility of my returning to the past.

Adjusting to the choice that I had made, the choice for growth, would be a different kind of life activity. For the moment, I was glad that the decision-making period was over. Acting on the decision would be easier than making it.

The Act

On Thursday, February 1, I was prepared to inform the college president of my decision to leave. He was not in that day, so I made an appointment for the following morning. I already had decided, in consultation with both of my sons, that the decision was independent of any other consideration between me and the college now or in the past, that it was not negotiable, and that it needed to be done with grace.

The president took my overcoat and I closed the door to his office. I began by telling him that it was going to be an important conversation. I said that I had decided to leave the college, and that I had come for three reasons: to explain why I was leaving, to ask for his blessing, and to let him know that I was not withdrawing my support from the college which had been a good home for my professional career in higher education and for a major part of my chronological life. I told him that I knew that my resignation would come as a surprise and that I wanted to give him time to think about what he would like me to do before I left and to tell me what he needed to know in order to facilitate a smooth transition in the international center and its programs.

I gave him an abbreviated version of my story. I had already told him in early December, when he and his wife graciously brought dinner to our home, that my journey was a journey of the soul, so he was not completely unprepared. He also had a college degree in theology, along with his degree in philosophy, so I knew that he would understand the language of calls and missions and surrender. I told him, as I would tell everyone else at the college, that I was not going away from the college, but going toward something else. That was a subtle point. It was complicated at each telling by my inability to say where it was that I was going.

The president made a few quiet attempts to suggest that I stay attached to the college in any one of a variety of ways until I got reestablished in a future position, but I did not accept those offers and was sure that he felt my resolve. Neither of us made any further try at following that line of thinking. I told him that I would be leaving in two weeks, but that I had spent the previous three weeks getting everything in the international center and its programs in impeccable order and that I would lead transition meetings and leave detailed instructions for those who took over from me so that nothing would get left undone during the first few weeks and months of their new work. He knew me well enough to trust that that would happen; I had done it before when it had been time to turn over various programs.

That actually was the perfect time for me to turn the international center over to someone else. Everything was under control and we had learned that we had been awarded the large grant from the philanthropy whose grant request I had written from my hospital bed and had shepherded through to the finish during those first two very long days after I had returned home from the second surgery. Not only was everything in order but the members of the staff had been working at a distance for three months by then and they had developed a level of confidence in their own decision making, even though we conversed almost daily by telephone. That was an ideal time to transition them from their dependence on my existence to their paths as young managers themselves. I spent a lot of time with them, helping them to see their own capabilities and to learn how to develop their own careers. They were outstanding contributors to the program and before I left I made sure to recommend raises for them and to protect their positions as much as I could.

The president said that he would like to take the weekend to absorb what I had told him that Friday, and I certainly agreed to that, assuring him that I had told no one else at the college, and would not until he had been able to assimilate the information. I always had been loyal to the presidents of the college. I was not a believer in the "we-they" mentality to which some of my faculty colleagues subscribed, and chose instead always to let principle guide my choices and advice. Being loyal to the president did not mean always agreeing with the president; it meant giving him my honest opinion on all issues, even if I knew that he would not agree with, and sometimes would not appreciate, that opinion. It also meant giving him that opinion in private, and supporting whatever decisions he ultimately made.

I told him that it was important to me that my leaving reflect a positive ending between the college and me. I had been an important player in the life of the college for a long time and I wanted my departure to reflect the same grace that I had attempted to bring to the college during those years. Certainly there had been the usual kinds of professional disagreements on occasion over such a long period of time, but I had no professional secrets from the president and I made sure that he always knew what I was thinking.

That night, Dave took me out for dinner at my favorite Italian restaurant. It was interesting to look at my monthly calendar for February. There was nothing blocked in for that first weekend, only the name of the college. I spent most of that weekend at the college getting all of my projects in order for my successor. The calendar boxes representing the days in the following two weeks were solidly covered with tiny written-in schedules for meetings. The weekend between simply said "college move."

On the Monday following my announcement to the president, we met again. He asked if I had changed my mind about anything. I assured him that I had not. He said that he recognized that it would do no good to make any offers for me to stay, but if he thought that I would listen to them, he would make them. That was much like calling someone first to check their availability before sending them a formal, written invitation. I just smiled. Nothing could have changed my mind that day. He also said that he understood that sometimes it is important for a person to act quickly. All in all he was very gracious about the situation. Gracious, but quick to act himself, as a president must be.

The Response

I asked that the college president wait to announce my resignation until I had had a chance personally to tell my staff, especially Sarah and Denise and also to give me time to personally inform those administrators with whom I had worked so closely over the years. The hardest person of all to tell was Sarah. That graceful young woman from Hohhut, China had been with me four years before when the international center was just a fledgling center. We changed sheets together in the guest house, washed dishes together in the bathroom sink, wrote memos together, pondered Chinese responses together. I helped her understand the etiquette of American professional life; she helped me to understand the etiquette of the Chinese culture. She often said that she was envious of the education that I personally gave to the Chinese students and faculty, and that she wished she could be my student instead of my assistant. The truth was that she was far more than an assistant to me. She was a partner, a teacher herself, and much like a daughter.

I told Sarah my news first. She came to me like a child for a hug and she cried. I put my arms around that lovely, gentle being, that daughter, and hugged her. "Sarah," I said, "this is only for a little while. When I find out what I am supposed to do with my life, I will come for you. I will find you. Wherever you are, I will find you." And then to add some lightness to this overwhelmingly powerful good-bye, I added, "Except please, Sarah, don't go back to China. Don't make me try to find you among all the people there."

Next I told Denise, who also was Chinese, but from Taiwan not Mainland China. I had been very impressed with her resume when I had first read it and had tried to get in touch with her when I had an opening in the international center. When we finally connected, she informed me that she had just taken another position. I asked her to call me if she was ever available again. Fortunately, both for me and for the international center, she did call later and I hired her immediately. Several months after hiring Denise, I began my journey, and she and I communicated from then on by phone, fax, and e-mail. She was the consummate professional both when I was there and when we were at a distance. I never worried about any of her assignments. She was a delight to work with, a font of positive energy in her own right. Now, I was telling her that I was leaving and that she was going to be okay without me. And, she was.

There were five other people at the college whom I needed to tell myself. I spoke with two of them that afternoon. Two of the others were at lunch; the third was not in that day. The two who were at lunch, both men, burst into my office a few hours later. They had just had a meeting with the president and had been informed of my resignation. They were aghast, incredulous, astounded, hurt, and angry. Why hadn't I told them first? Why hadn't I consulted with them while I was making the decision? Why couldn't I wait six months? What would they do without me?

I told them that I had had a very strong intuition that it was time for me to move on, that there was something else for me to do, and that I needed to get ready for that. Both of those men understood the spiritual. The three of us had been like the three musketeers of interpersonal teaching; each of us viewed teaching as a spiritual mission. Regularly, we were three who were heralded by the students as excellent and favored teachers at the college. All three of us believed that the purpose of education was the development of individual human potential for the benefit of human kind. All three of us were motivators. I tried to explain to them that I was not leaving our joint mission, merely the place in which it was being carried out. It was with mixed feelings that they left my office that afternoon.

It always is easier for the person who is moving forward, harder for the ones who stay.

Done

As I organized my projects, I taught as many people as I could about the international center so that there would be strength throughout the college for its continuance. Unfortunately my two colleagues were threatened somehow by that openness, a management style of mine: no secrets, all information available to everyone. They became angry and actually boycotted informative meetings that they needed in order to help support the center. One of them eventually came around and took part in the transition; the other has not spoken to me since. That was not what I would have wanted for my last week, but I had learned over and over again throughout that adventure that I was not in charge. My departure from the college was so unexpected, by us all, and so out of character for me, that it affected different people in many different ways.

I personally called all of the major donors to the program and explained my decision. With each phone call I emphasized that I was not going away from the college, but on to something else. I became accustomed to the inevitable question about what that something else was and I answered honestly that my decision had been a leap of faith, a complete surrender. The major donors to my program included some well known names in the United States. One of them admonished me for acting without a strategy; another wondered if I was going to enter a convent;

a third thought that I was responding to the life-threatening blood clots and their possible connection to my frequent travels to China. All of them thought that my decision was terrible news for the college, but characteristically they supported my decision.

I also personally called all of my colleagues in China to assure them of the continuance of the international program and to thank them for their friendship and their support. I happened to make these phone calls on Chinese New Year, the year of the horse, and so was able to wish them and their families a Happy New Year as well. I told them that their friendship had been so important to me that I wanted them to hear of my departure from the college in my own voice even though we were halfway around the world from each other. We had been together so often in China and so often in thought that the miles no longer made any difference. That was the world toward which we were heading; that was the world that my international center was helping to create.

The alumni started to call. Their first concern was that I was okay. Calls or e-mails from Singapore, Europe, China, South America, the East Coast, and the Bay Area followed one another as the news got around, wonderfully supportive communications. Books, cards, and invitations for lunch came next. And then, one day, early in my last week at the college, came one of the saddest communications that a teacher can get: on January 22 one of my former students—33 years old, married, the father of a three-year-old son—had died. I called his wife and only got the answering machine, but left a message. Early the next week I called again and found her at home. I wanted to tell her how special her husband had been to me, to us all, but she was ill, exhausted, overcome with loss and the best that I could do was to offer to come and help her. She was not ready. Her husband, my student, a young man who knew that he was on a journey, had died in the middle of the night—*from a blood clot to the lung*.

By eight o'clock the morning following my second meeting with the president, before the monthly all-employee meeting, an e-mail informing the college of my resignation had been sent to the entire campus. In the e-mail, the president stated that I had created the most innovative and best international program in the nation and that it would be hard to replace me. He announced that after I had left, one of the deans would guide the program during its transition to a new leader. The next two weeks were a blur of activity, a return to my pre-surgery long, long days, the usual many meetings, the preparations for the transition.

During the weekend, I cleared out my office, organized my files, and prepared instructions for the staff and the new leadership of the program. Ben drove down from Sacramento to help me move the boxes. My sons had grown up on that campus. They had joined me on their school holidays, had done their homework on my office computer, had visited classes that I taught. Ben, following in his mom's footsteps, has taught Business Law, Business Ethics, and Political Science at the college for several years now. Dave did everything imaginable to support my work at the college, from carpentry work on evenings and weekends to computer modeling long into the night to taking the Chinese visitors on outings every weekend of the first two years, and frequently in the last two years.

Twenty-three years is a long time. One third of a person's life is a long time. I had been blessed in so many ways. My professional life had been one of those blessings. And it had been bound inextricably to the life of my family. The commanding intuition demanded a big price. Nothing short of the physical events of the fall, the intuition, its corresponding sadness, and my lesson that I must handle the experience by myself could have convinced me to leave the college and my life there.

My last official act at the college was to visit the Faculty Senate in order to say good-bye to my colleagues. I owed them an explanation. I also owed them my gratitude. Those individuals had not been hired for their research abilities, for which most teachers in the country were hired. Instead they were hired for their love of and talent for teaching. Most of them were on a mission of some kind. The professor who had hired me, now emeritus, was in the room, so was one of my former students, now a professor in her own right. I acknowledged at that time the personal contribution to my life of each of the professors with whom I had worked: one who was a brilliant writer; another who was a gifted logician; the man who was a skilled leader; the former dean who taught me about being an administrator; a formidable adversary who had studied philosophy as an undergraduate: dedicated teachers, honorable human beings, bodhisattvas all, individuals who would remain behind to help others on their paths.

Beyond my explanation and my gratitude I needed to remind them of the importance of their work and to let them know that my leaving in no way denigrated the work that we all had done together and that they would continue to do. It mattered to me that my leaving did not cause them to question their work.

With that, I left the meeting, walked across the oak-studded campus with the lovely floral arrangement that my colleagues had given me, spoke with the Chinese donor who earlier in the day had come to a combination Valentine's Day/farewell party given by the Chinese visitors, said good-bye, closed my door, and left the international center that we had created four years earlier.

It was significant that it was Valentine's Day, for my work at the college had been a labor of love, and my leaving the college had been a response from the heart.

No Need To Look Back

The difference between my vision and the vision of the college was confirmed in the weeks following my departure. I was told that the international center might be disassembled and the various parts distributed to other departments. The body of the center, its physical complex, was to be given to a department that knew little about the intricacies of the international program. The soul of the center, its creative international programs, had already been given to the very people who had claimed that the primary mission of the college was the education of the traditional students.

Like many of us, I learned life lessons from my parents. One of the lessons that I had learned long ago from my father was that upon leaving a position it was important not to stay involved. The reason for that was that continued involvement by the former leader confuses the transition of the staff to the new leader and ultimately makes it more difficult for the new leader to establish his or her own rhythm and goals. Knowing that, I have had very little contact with the international center since my departure.

I did not look back. My physician asked me if there was any seed of regret about my decision. My immediate answer was no. My answer was to remain the same into the future. I have neither looked back nor thought much about the college or the international center, other than to write this story.

One of the most beautiful passages in all literature comes from Martin Buber's *I and Thou*. Buber, an existentialist like Kierkegaard, describes in eloquent language our realm of choice as a swirling cosmos into which we must thrust our hands and grab our destinies. Once done, all of the possibilities fall into one of two groups, the chosen and the non-chosen. All of the non-chosen alternatives are now delusion and are not to be considered further. The chosen has become the task, and all of the force and energy of the non-chosen must be directed to the chosen task.

I have loved that passage for a long time. It is strong language, and it spoke to me of 100% commitment. Once we have made a choice, we need to give it all of our energy and focus. I had made a choice to move on to something beyond the college. That something was to be my task. The choice to move on had been my choice. I was responsible for that choice. It was time to focus all of my energy on the beyond.

That did not mean that I had lost my love for the college or the international center. It simply meant that I was moving ahead again on my journey. Everyone who has been significant to us in our lives has contributed to who we are. No significant person is forgotten and in memory each one can be pulled as close to us now as they were in the past. Love does not end with time. The college of my professional life, my colleagues, my students, the alumni, the donors, and my international partners all were part of my being. I did not need a mystical experience to know that they were a permanent part of my life. I did not need to look back because I carried all of them within me.

HEALING

Leap Of Faith

When I made the decision to leave the college, I put my life in the hands of the spiritual universe. Acting on the intuition had been a leap of faith. I had tried to make the journey be a journey of reason, a rational psychological analysis, but at some point—maybe always—it had become a journey of the spirit. Reason had been useful, essential even, in the process, but it was not the motivating power in the process. The power came from somewhere else. I had no idea where the power was going to lead me, but I was filled with joy and exuberance to be on the adventure.

I had not been afraid of the leap when I finally made the decision. William James, the American psychologist, says that there are two kinds of people when it comes to faith: those who are afraid of being duped and those who are afraid of missing the boat. I was clearly one of the latter. I was not afraid that I had been duped—either by my own analysis or by the universe—nor was I afraid of whatever might appear on the adventure. More important to me: I did not want to miss the opportunity for growth, did not want to miss the boat.

As high-minded as all of that sounded, my decision might have seemed to some to be a pretty gutsy decision: it was conceivable that I would never "do" again and that I could lose everything that I had. Stories abound of individuals who once were prominent and who disappeared from the world, went into seclusion. Occasionally I wondered who the bag ladies had been in their past lives. It never occurred to me that I could disappear from the world, that I could become a bag lady. My travel bag overflowed with symbols and guidelines and a renewed sense of freedom, with optimism, trust and boundless energy.

I knew that, having met personal and societal standards for adult success, I no longer was bound by the standard rules of the game for those in mid life. I had realized that at my brother's vineyard years earlier when I had signed the "Summer Agreement" that had encouraged us all to move forward and not just to "drone on." I, of course, was still bound by moral rules, but not by rules for outward success in the world.

At lunch one day with a former student, an intellectually gifted, high-achieving young woman, I got a sense of timing. After quizzing me intensely and earnestly listening to my responses, she said, "I think I understand, but for people my age, watching someone like you just give up a career is threatening. We are working to get where you are and you are giving that up!" And, it turns out that that is part of this story: do we continue doing what we have done before, perhaps repeating an earlier life and its lessons over and over again, like a stick in an eddy, or are we always on a journey to parts unknown, finding more of our world and more of ourselves along the way?

Whether the intuition merely had been a catalyst to end the ennui of a life journey suspended in time, or had momentously signaled a change in level of conscious life, I was not sure at that time, but I treated it as the latter. Now, from beyond the decision making process—the response to the intuition—the decision seemed even less like a difficult step ahead on the same path and more like the end of that path itself. If the leap had been to a new consciousness rather than just to a new step on a career path, I would need to proceed accordingly. New levels of consciousness were about Being, not about Doing.

I knew that there was a great difference between Being, Doing, and Having, and that who I was as a person was not the same as what I did or what I had. My decision to leave the college had involved all three of those aspects of my life. First, it left me without income. (Having) Second, it left me with no clear work in the world. (Doing) Finally, it challenged my sense of who I was (Being), because in answering the question "Who are you?" I could not fall back on either what I did or what I had.

I was comfortable with addressing the question of Being because I knew at some very deep level that the journey I was on required that who I *was* would determine what I *did* in the future and what I *had* in the future. I would need to be very clear about who I was before I once again entered the worlds of Doing and Having, if that was where I was going. My only choice seemed just to Be—and to observe what happened.

Being

Several things happened in the months that followed Valentine's Day and my departure from the college. Almost immediately the sadness vanished, as would be expected if, indeed, it was linked to my earlier questioning of the intuition and its "call to adventure." The sadness was replaced by internal energy and exuberance. My focus, usually direct and intense, widened but did not appear to soften or blur as might be expected. I found myself in a state of eager anticipation, of readiness. I was completely open to what might come.

Along with this energy and widened focus came the feelings of acceptance and appreciation, acceptance of whatever came my way and appreciation for whatever it was, as it was—with one exception: I was not yet ready to come down from Maslow's mountain peak. There had been a connection between me and something very deep and powerful. I wanted to remain close to that. The only moves that I made to control my universe were those that brought me closer to passionate transcendent experiences and those that distanced me from negative, passive ones.

I had no agenda, no goal, no strategic plan. I just *was*.

For months I alternated between observing my own emotional responses—which put a measure of distance between me and the emotions—and setting aside my rational mind in order simply to experience life without any judgment.

Beyond my rational mind, I saw the fallen red leaves in circular array beneath the trees. I saw the silhouette of barren branches against the late afternoon sun. I caught my breath at the brilliance and purity of the new light green leaves. I inhaled the perfumes of blossoms both tiny and large. The days passed and I joined them, not once categorizing their movement into seasons.

The water behind my home changed from dark blue to turquoise to green, once to a rust brown, and often to an inky black in the night. The surface slid from smooth glassiness to windswept white caps. I felt the sun on my face and the wind in my hair. I wore t-shirts and shorts, and then parkas and gloves.

I stood quietly on the path that circled the park, intoxicated with the color of green that filled my entire visual field. Before my eyes the fog silently cascaded over the Pacific Range. I walked in the rain and in the sunshine, in the heat and the cold, the day and the night. I walked with Professor Higgins by my side, and I walked alone.

I absorbed everything through my body and nothing through my thoughts. I listened intently to the metronomic sounds of the cat sleeping in the sunshine. I watched humming birds and ducks and spiders and dogs and barely visible insects. I responded to the rhythm of life by matching it in my soul. Gradually, I healed in body and spirit and gradually I came closer to the essence of my being.

At first, the loneliness was a frequent visitor. I watched it come and go; I let it come and go. As the days passed, the loneliness lessened and was replaced by an immense sense of gratitude and joy.

Those solitary, non-rational, physical moments, which were predominant in my life for months, were interspersed with visits with my students, friends, and former colleagues, and those were precious moments. As before, I focused intently on what these individuals had to say, on their joys and concerns. I shared their lives with them, and told them openly about my new experiences. In the best Hegelian tradition, I became a conduit between the depth of the universe and the people around me. The conversations always moved in the direction of their life journeys. The people and the conversations were an immensely valuable part of my life.

And so it was that the surgeon, with whom I had a few more appointments that year, slipped into a special part of my life where resided those who had been significant to me but who could no longer stay with me, protected by my gratefulness for their having been a part of my life.

The months provided the answer to my questions: I thought only rarely about seeking professional work. I had little need for money. I never worried about status or felt unimportant in the world. And, I knew the value of my contributions to individuals who entered or remained in my life. I experienced the ground of my being as continual joy that ranged from a warm fullness to a passionate appreciation of the world in which I lived.

I walked with lightness.

About The Author

Professor Harvey holds a PhD in Philosophy from Stanford University and is Emeritus Professor and Dean of Menlo College, a small private college in Northern California. She is an award-winning teacher who has created many unique courses in Philosophy, Psychology, and the Humanities. Dr. Harvey is an experienced motivational speaker, known for her talent for simplifying and personalizing the big philosophical issues and introducing them through stories.

Currently Professor Harvey is president of *Life Journey Seminars* which mentors individuals in small group settings and hosts philosophical salons focusing on ethical, political, and social issues.

Diane Harvey lives in Northern California with her husband, David. They have two adult sons: Will Harvey, PhD and Ben Harvey, JD. Besides her teaching and writing, Professor Harvey enjoys skiing, scuba diving, traveling, and all of the family pets.

Lightning Source UK Ltd.
Milton Keynes UK
UKOW041446270513

211304UK00002B/450/A